SHORT CUTS

INTRODUCTIONS TO FILM STUDIES

FILM AND THE NATURAL ENVIRONMENT

ELEMENTS AND ATMOSPHERES

ADAM O'BRIEN

WALLFLOWER

LONDON and NEW YORK

A Wallflower Press book
Published by
Columbia University Press
Publishers Since 1893
New York • Chichester, West Sussex
cup.columbia.edu

A complete CIP record is available from the Library of Congress

ISBN 978-0-231-18265-2 (pbk. : alk. paper)
ISBN 978-0-231-85110-7 (e-book)

Columbia University Press books are printed on permanent and durable acid-free paper.
Printed in the United States of America

Cover image: Still the Water (2014) © Soda Pictures

CONTENTS

ACKNOWLEDGEMENTS

I wrote this book since joining the Department of Film, Theatre & Television at the University of Reading, and can only hope that it reflects some of the qualities which have made this such an ideal place for sharing and exploring ideas about cinema. At Reading, Lisa Purse, John Gibbs, Tamara Courage and Stefan Solomon deserve particular thanks. Michael Malay (Bristol) offered some typically astute suggestions, Alastair Phillips (Warwick) recommended an excellent book at an opportune moment, and Yoram Allon (Commissioning Editor at Wallflower Press) was patient and encouraging from start to finish.

I am doubly fortunate to have a loving family surrounded by *more* loving family, and am grateful for how much they all support my work. Roddy, Joseph and Ruth are the distractions one could hope for, and Rebecca continues to know and help me in countless ways.

INTRODUCTION

Is *Titanic* (1997) a film about nature? We might instinctively say that it is, on the grounds that the film's drama is based on a catastrophe suffered at sea, instigated by a force beyond human, social influence. Until we recall that *Titanic* places a heavy emphasis on the culpability of certain people, and wonder whether that makes it a work less about nature. But would the film's meanings, effects and pleasures be the same had the disaster been distinctively man-made (a declaration of war, for example)? And if *Titanic* seems to be positing nature as an antagonist, distinct from social phenomena such as capitalism, class and technology, does that mean that the iceberg *represents* nature? What about the wind which blows against Jack (Leonardo DiCaprio) and Rose (Kate Winslet) as they stand at the bow of the ship, and which enables Rose's fantasy of flying? How can one natural feature take meaningful priority over another? Where does nature begin and end?

Raymond Williams suggests that since nature is a word 'which carries, over a very long period, many of the major variations of human thought [...] it is necessary to be especially aware of its difficulty' (2014: 189). 'Nature', 'natural' and related terms have received much interrogation, and rightly so; understanding the divide between 'natural' and 'unnatural' is an activity of huge political, ethical, scientific and philosophical complexity. Likewise 'human' and 'non-human', 'environment' and 'landscape', 'local' and 'global', 'object' and 'organism', among others. The language and images we use to conjure up worldly phenomena not traceable to human design is fraught with shortcomings, oversights and contradictions. Kate Soper gives a sense of this in her excellent introduction to the topic, *What is Nature?*:

> Nature is both machine and organism, passive matter and vitalist agency. It is represented as both savage and noble, polluted and wholesome, lewd and innocent, carnal and pure, chaotic and ordered. Conceived as a feminine principle, nature is equally lover, mother and virago; a source of sensual delight, a nurturing bosom, a site of treacherous violation. Sublime and pastoral, indifferent to human purposes and willing servant of them, nature awes as she consoles, strikes terror as she pacifies, presents herself as both the best of friends and the worst of foes. (1995: 71)

Soper brings some order to the confusion by proposing three conceptual versions of nature: the 'metaphysical' (how humankind distinguishes itself from an 'other'), the 'realist' (structures and processes, subject to scientific study, which influence the planet) and the 'lay' (observable features of the non-urban and non-industrial world, familiar and available to common experience). Throughout this book, I will largely be following Soper's third concept, and have settled upon the term 'natural environment' to more clearly distinguish the topic from philosophical explorations of naturality. In other contexts, I have sometimes avoided using the terms 'nature' and 'the environment', nervous of how they, taken together, can conjure up a certain warm-blanket complacency; but this book is not a work of eco-critical theory, and its terms are designed to be accessible and far reaching. As Soper explains, 'talk of the countryside and its "natural" flora and fauna may be loose, but it still makes discriminations that we would want to observe' (1995: 20).

There are other reasons for what may be considered a naïve definition of nature. Taking seriously the work of creative artists – composers, poets, painters, novelists, sculptors, playwrights, photographers, filmmakers – often involves acknowledging that *something* has turned their attention away from human forms and subjects; something has allowed them to re-contextualise human experience in a manner which we find arresting and enlightening. 'Insofar as nature is something and not nothing, then it must be something encountered in a particular way, at a finite place, for somebody' (Mules 2014: 18) – or, I would add, for a work of art. But such encounters are not simply a case of biophilic or nature-loving impulses. The stance taken up by any given artist may be one of awe, fear, hubris, naivety, irony, curiosity or any number of alternatives; *Titanic*, for example, could be said to answer to almost all of these. There is not a genre or mode of natural-environment art, but rather a common urge amongst a great many (deeply dissimilar) artists to acknowledge the world as something more than a stage for social transactions.

These are big ideas with which to begin a short book. But they are ideas which have been, until recently, surprisingly muted in academic film studies, and so deserve to be set out boldly and starkly. Much has been written about the medium's crucial engagement with key aspects of modernity – such as urbanisation, mechanised warfare and global capitalism – to the extent that film is thought to be tied *absolutely* to twentieth-century concerns. But filmmakers, like other artists, are invariably interested in the way humankind understands its relationship with the non-human world; and film, like other art forms, brings with it *particular* affordances in this regard.

For example, the movement in time of snow and rain, birds and beasts, streams and waterfalls, is something that painters and poets, unlike filmmakers, struggle to communicate or represent. On the other hand, a filmmaker will find it difficult to deploy metaphor or invoke subjective impressions of the natural world – which is one reason why nature writing is deeply resistant to film adaptation. Derek Bousé has written that 'film and television are about movement, action and dynamism; nature is generally not' (2000: 4). This is a simplistic reduction of all three, but still a useful reminder of the potentially awkward fit between the tendencies of moving-image media and some important qualities of the natural world.

Of course all artistic media could be said to produce their own 'awkward fit' with non-human nature, and given the centuries-long traditions of environmental imagining in literary, theatrical, musical and fine arts, it is important not to fall into the trap of thinking that cinema came too late to the party, or that it is doomed to repeat the conventions of, for example, landscape painting, the Romantic sublime, pastoralism or wilderness discourse. These extant modes are not irrelevant to cinema, but they have not determined the trajectory of its environmental imagination. To properly appreciate the subject of film and the natural environment, such terms are useful, but not necessarily more useful than neorealism, film noir, mise-en-scène and montage. A painting of an iceberg is one thing; an establishing shot of an iceberg, however graphically similar, is quite another thing. Jack and Rose on the bow of the *Titanic* comes to us by way of *this* medium's forms, conventions and mysteries.

This volume stems from the belief that nature is of profound interest to a great many filmmakers and film scholars, even if it is not always prioritised as a subject in and of itself. Throughout the book, I will discuss genres and national cinemas, theories and theorists, directors and critics, many of which will already be familiar to readers who have engaged with film studies to some extent. I will not be focusing my attention on an overlooked body of work, but rather an overlooked approach or strand of thinking. I will not be limiting the discussion to films which thematise nature, and will deliberately cast a broad geographical and historical net.

There are still some necessary limits, however. I will focus on fictional narrative cinema, not only because this is likely to be of the most immediate interest to the greatest number of readers, but also because experimental and documentary cinema both have relatively distinct traditions of environment-engaged scholarship dedicated to them. (Animal studies is another related field to which I cannot quite do justice in this book.) Concentrating on films which explicitly set out to creatively tell stories will also lend the overall a discussion a greater consistency and coherence, allowing key ideas and motifs to recur and develop as the book progresses. The subtitle, *Elements and Atmospheres,* is an attempt to capture the book's dual focus, alluding to both interpretive analysis and environmental subjects.

Chapter 1 takes a brief tour through three key sub-categories of the discipline – film theory, film history and film criticism – and suggests a number of ways in which the natural environment has already been a present, if not central, concern in film studies. Chapter 2 revisits some of the most important constituents of film narrative, such as point of view, causality and characterisation, and teases out the sometimes subtle ways in which film storytelling can draw on natural phenomena. The subject of Chapter 3 is film genre; more specifically, how the natural environment often plays an important role in establishing and developing the horizons of a given genre's 'world', and how this manifests itself in the example of film noir. And Chapter 4 turns to the question of national cinemas, focusing on Japanese film as an example of how and when an environmental focus might reveal important continuities (and discontinuities) in a particular country's body of work.

This is not a polemical book. Instead, each chapter occupies and demonstrates a position – or series of positions – from which readers may want to explore further the topic of cinema and nature. That said, this is not simply an exercise; I write in the genuine belief that environmental questions still have a great deal more to contribute to film studies, and that there are strong ethical and intellectual reasons for attending more closely to the natural environments of narrative cinema. To this end, certain recurring questions animate the book as a whole; they are implicit touchstones, oriented towards whichever film we are faced with:

– Why does this film in particular seem to demand an environmentally informed analysis or interpretation? And in responding to that demand, are we simply describing and summarising the film's features – its images, themes and narrative – or are we genuinely working towards an enriched understanding of its form and meaning?

– Has this film invoked or explored the natural environment in ways which are distinctive to, or deeply characteristic of, the medium?

– How does all this come to fruition in particular details, moments and sequences?

To return to the example of *Titanic*, we could say that the iceberg collision is an unavoidable reason for reading the film as one concerned with nature, but also that it poses a challenge of how to move towards something more nuanced than crude nature/technology binaries. One way to confront this challenge is to explore the particular use it makes of cinema's most distinctive capabilities – such as the manipulation of duration, regular shifts in scale, sound/image dynamics and star presence. This would then enable us, for example, to think about the famous 'king of the world' moment in more refined terms. Why do we not see Jack's point of view? Does he (or the film's viewer) know where in the world he is at this moment? What are the implications of him howling like a wild animal, whilst proclaiming himself king? And why does Rose process the same experience quite differently, as one of flight?

In response to my opening question, then, the following book is *not* an attempt to find which films are 'about' nature, but rather an invitation to consider how some films negotiate a compelling relationship with their environmental subjects and objects. 'If the language of nature is mute', wrote Theodor Adorno, 'art seeks to make this muteness eloquent' (1997: 106). Cinema has demonstrated a capacity for such eloquence in a great many ways and means, and the following chapters have been written in an attempt to do some justice to that wealth and diversity.

1 FILM STUDIES AND THE NATURAL ENVIRONMENT

This chapter is an introduction to the existing body of work, within film studies, that addresses the medium's relationship with the natural environment. I will begin by offering an overview of the particular subfield of ecocritical film studies, before surveying some of the less direct engagements with environmental subject matter in film theory, film history and film criticism, to indicate how these disciplinary approaches can – and often do – incorporate a considered awareness of the natural world. What follows is not an evaluative or critical engagement with the work in question, but rather a journey through some important and illuminating writers, writings and themes. Nadia Bozak writes that 'cinema is, and always has been, environmentally determined and determining' (2011: 4), but questions of environmental form and meaning have, until recently, emerged rather sporadically in English-language film studies; I hope the following summaries will help interested readers to follow the threads.

Environmental film studies

While the mid-twentieth century saw the beginnings of what we might call mainstream environmentalism, it was some decades after this before questions of environmental engagement became firmly entrenched in arts and humanities scholarship. Disciplines which traditionally seemed to have a strong human focus – history, economics, literature – have been enriched by an increasingly sophisticated exploration of humans' embeddedness in the non-human world. For every subfield (such as environmental history or eco-philosophy) there are of course many important predecessors stretching back decades and even centuries, but the widespread and sustained concern with environmental questions has been a relatively recent trend, of which film studies can be said to be a part. Researchers interested in exploring cinema's relationship with the natural world will find themselves mainly consulting work written since the start of the twenty-first century.

One strand of this work has been concerned with cinema's relative contribution to environmentalism as a political and ethical cause. Some writers on this subject proceed from the understanding that humans' relationship to their natural surroundings is a matter of urgent concern, and that film can and does play an influential role in the maintenance of that relationship. Questions of responsibility, stewardship, sustainability and representation are likely to predominate in this work, more so than film-theoretical or aesthetic concerns (although the distinction is by no means absolute). In part because of its widespread influence, American cinema has been the subject of a considerable amount of this kind of study; see, for example, the work of David Ingram (2000) and Pat Brereton (2005; 2015), while Robin L. Murray and Joseph K. Heumann (2009; 2012) have thoroughly chronicled environmental trends and cycles in popular film. Chinese cinema has also been an area of focus (Lu and Mi 2009), not least because that country has experienced, and initiated, particularly extreme environmental transformations during its recent accelerated modernisation.

Some of the principles and key methodological traits of the environmentalist approach are clearly evident in a piece by Roberto Forns-Broggi, 'Ecocinema and "Good Life" in Latin America' (2013), which describes and praises two documentaries about environmental injustice in Latin America, *When Clouds Clear* (2008) and *The Devil Operation* (2010). The first feature we might notice in this essay is the use of the term 'ecocinema' in the title, a move based on the idea that a vast body of work can be delineated, one which 'reflects a consciousness about both fruitful and problematic relations with natural life' (2013: 185). The case studies are discussed as exemplars of a broader wave of environmentally and politically progressive work emerging from Ecuador and Bolivia in recent years, in and beyond cinema. Where the films are evaluated by Forns-Broggi, it is primarily in terms of their instrumentality, their usefulness to a cause. No mention is made of the films' aesthetic strategies or their textual qualities, and the author's points of reference are predominantly works of 'green' cultural studies rather than film theory or criticism.

This is not to say that politically-charged writing on film and the environment is necessarily carried out in isolation from the 'conventional' concerns of film studies (narrative, mise-en-scène, technology, reception), but Forns-Broggi's writing can certainly be said to occupy one end of a spectrum; his primary interests are political rather than aesthetic. Another notable feature of his essay is its tendency to place the films in a media – rather than an exclusively filmic – context. An increasing amount of work relevant to environmental film studies is similarly oriented towards media; the reasons behind this shift are of course many and complex, and for a more thorough understanding, readers are encouraged to explore collections such as *Ecosee: Image, Rhetoric, Nature, Greening the Media* (Drobin and Morey 2009) and *Ecomedia: Key Issues* (Rust *et al.* 2016).

If one strand of scholarship on film and the environment can be said to explore cinema's role in a socio-political struggle toward greater ecological responsibility, a slightly different approach is adopted by writers such as Nadia Bozak, Adrian Ivakhiv, Sean Cubitt, Kristi McKim and Scott MacDonald, and is perhaps best represented by an excellent collection of essays edited by Anat Pick and Guinevere Narraway, *Screening Nature: Cinema Beyond the Human* (2013). Such work is by no means apolitical, but the question it raises is not so much how film can be produced and circulated in environmentally progressive ways, but rather how best we might respond to film's particular and distinctive engagement with the natural environment. In the same way that important patterns and insights can be found in the medium's relationship with the female body, historical narrative, childhood, national identity and domesticity, for example, so the natural environment has been a privileged subject of film which warrants close critical attention. Such an approach will typically avoid treating case studies primarily as rhetorical or ideological texts, and will more likely attend to the aesthetic particulars of exemplary work.

This broadly describes the way in which Nadia Bozak writes about Werner Herzog (2011), Adrian Ivakhiv writes about Andrei Tarkovsky (2013), Guinevere Narraway writes about Rose Lowder (2013), and Kristi McKim writes about Woody Allen (2013). McKim, for example, does not argue that

Allen's films provide any kind of social purpose with regard to how they envision and narrate characters' relationship with their environment; however, she does make a very convincing case that the director of *Manhattan* (1979), *Hannah and Her Sisters* (1986) and *Match Point* (2005) is unusually and consistently thoughtful when it comes to the deployment of weather – particularly rain – in his films. Drawing on interviews with Allen, and her own close textual analysis, McKim demonstrates how Allen's characters invariably seek shelter from the rain, complementing the inwardness and self-reflection they tend to practise (2013: 117). She is writing in the context of a broader study of weather in cinema, one which tends to emphasise matters of style, narrative and interpretation ahead of environmental politics, but also one which nevertheless hopes to model 'a perceptual sensitivity towards the atmosphere that could have political implications for our current and future ecosystems' (2013: 4).

Nadia Bozak could be said to adopt a reverse approach. In *The Cinematic Footprint: Lights, Camera, Natural Resources* (2011) she takes as her starting point film's material entanglement with natural resources such as sunlight and fossil fuels, and moves *from* this precondition of the medium towards imaginative interpretations of a range of films and stylistic tropes. Bozak's approach, for example, allows her to compare how celluloid cinema and digital video provide different opportunities for filmmakers to document resource-driven wars; she also contemplates the long take as a gesture which makes 'the consumptive foundations of cinema conspicuous' (2011: 132). Bozak's examples are wonderfully various, and make a very strong (but non-prescriptive) case for cinema's inextricable relationship with natural energy and resources.

This is a common line of thinking within contemporary ecocritical writing; film is not (only) a recorder of natural subjects, but is itself closely bound up in ecological networks. While Bozak argues this with reference to film's direct reliance on material resources, others have made the argument using somewhat more abstract, philosophical terms. Sean Cubitt, for example, turns to Aristotle's conceptions of 'physis' (nature) and 'techne' (artistic craft) to argue for the ecological necessity of mediating images: 'Nature communicates with us as surely as we with it,' he writes, 'but to do so it must mediate' (2005: 134). In *Ecologies of the Moving Image* (2013), Adrian Ivakhiv draws on Sean Cubitt (as well as A. N. Whitehead, C. S. Pierce, Gilles Deleuze and Félix Guattari) to argue that the cinema-viewing experience is a particularly complex coming together of various ecological processes, in which we confront 'a world that is seemingly objective and material at one end, subjective and experiential at the other, and interperceptual in the middle: a world of subjects, objects and things in between' (2013: 11). Ivakhiv's theoretical apparatus is intricate and sometimes forbidding, but his work is valuable not least because of its ability to remind us of how uncannily 'natural' a film world can feel – alive, navigable, texturally rich, present to us but independent of us. His concluding thoughts on the films of Andrei Tarkovsky and Terrence Malick are especially illuminating; according to Ivakhiv, these filmmakers 'craft a mixture of total control and maximum release' (2013: 324), making the most of film's ability to let environmental phenomena transpire before it, without denying the medium's special propensity for sculpting new worlds from our existing one.

As already mentioned, many of these writers have been directly or indirectly influenced by an 'environmental turn' in the arts and humanities since around the turn of the twenty-first century, their research and analysis part of a broader movement known as ecocriticism. It is important to acknowledge, however, that writers in previous decades did of course raise insightful and perceptive questions about film and the environment, even if they did so in somewhat more isolated circumstances. Leo Braudy's 'The Genre of Nature', is one example; in an extensive survey of popular films of the 1980s and 1990s, he argues that 'the myths, metaphors and motifs of nature stand out, sometimes in shadows and shadings, but often in bold relief' (1998: 279). Braudy is perfectly aware of how complex and how historically contingent the idea of nature is, but nevertheless finds that it is a demonstrably important concern in a great many Hollywood films, from *Splash* (1984) and *Predator* (1987) to *Terminator 2* (1991) and *Jurassic Park* (1993). Writing more as a genre theorist than an environmental theorist, Braudy bypasses the knotty ethical and philosophical questions about the relative validity of nature as a concept, and instead turns his attention to observable patterns in what we might call Hollywood's discourse of nature. He observes, for example, the 'profoundly divided and even contradictory themes of nature as power and nature as victim' (1998: 296), and also the tendency for Hollywood films to characterise water as a source of energy and righteousness for their heroes. There is little attention to aesthetic detail in Braudy's essay;

rather it is a valuable thematic overview of popular cinema and its mobilisation of naturalness as an idea.

'Landscape in the Cinema' (1993), an essay by P. Adams Sitney, also warrants attention as an important forerunner in environmental film studies. The piece begins by noting that considerations of landscape and natural beauty have been awarded virtually no attention in critical writing on cinema. Sitney is ostensibly focused on the tradition of landscape spectacle, rather than broader conceptions of environment and ecology, but his far-reaching explorations of film history and technology, encompassing narrative and avant-garde cinema, makes for a very rich resource – not an argument or theory, but a sharply intelligent guide to the many techniques by which filmmakers 'share their surprise and excitement at the disjunctions and the meshings of the rhythms of the world and the temporality of the medium' (1993: 125). While bemoaning the general lack of attention to environmental film aesthetics, Sitney does point out that 'some of the first apologists for the cinema as an art made a point of the power and beauty of natural surroundings in film' (1993: 103), reminding us that early theorists of film were perhaps more attuned to the medium's environmental affinities than those writing in many subsequent decades. As we switch our attention from environmental film studies to the broader church of film theory, those 'first apologists' prove to be an appropriate point of departure.

Film theory

Robert Stam describes film theory as 'an evolving body of concepts designed to account for the cinema in all its dimensions' (2000: 6). When film theorists develop a particular account of the medium, they may choose to place their emphasis on one of its strongest tendencies, something that is not necessarily an absolutely defining feature, but is nevertheless suitably far-reaching. Examples of this include details of film technique (the cut, the long take), of film viewership (cognitive processes, psychoanalytic patterns of reception), or of film technology (CGI, camera mobility). Another path for film theory is an account of the medium by way of particular subjects to which it has been drawn, and for which it seems to have developed a peculiar and distinctive affinity; crowds, trains and human faces, for example, have been written about in such terms, as 'ingredients' with which film can somehow achieve its most essential capabilities – or at least subjects whose appearance in a film warrants special scrutiny and reflection. It is in this sense that the natural environment can be considered a concern for film theory.

A good place to begin reflecting on this is with early film theory, a body of work rich in examples of writers attempting to isolate and articulate the quintessential characteristics, and effects, of cinema. One of the most widely quoted responses to cinema in its very first years, 'On a Visit to the Kingdom of Shadows', was written by Maxim Gorky in 1896. In it, the Russian writer is particularly taken by the medium's unsettling combination of movement and silence, as well as its colourlessness. Early on in the piece, Gorky describes the 'Kingdom' thus: 'Everything there – the earth, the trees, the people, the water and the air – is dipped in monotonous grey. Grey rays of the sun across the grey sky, grey eyes in grey faces, and the leaves of the trees are ashen grey. It is not life but its shadow' (qtd. in Harding and Popple 1996: 5). The inclusiveness of Gorky's description is striking; the films he witnessed seem to have offered up entire worlds, made up of the same 'stuff' as ours, but all the more unsettling for that. He registers the fact that nature will inevitably be a part of almost any audio-visual record of a place and time, in ways that might well stretch beyond the intentions of the filmmaker, but also that such a record will have a simultaneous magical, *super*natural quality to it. Gorky was not a film theorist in the sense we generally use the term, but he was writing at a time when almost any account of film viewing had a kind of proto-theoretical currency. And he was one of many writers to describe the medium in distinctively non-anthropocentric terms.

Most famously, this was (loosely) theorised in France around the term 'photogénie', defined by Jean Epstein as 'any aspect of things, being or souls whose moral character is enhanced by filmic reproduction' (1981: 20). Sometimes the illustrative examples provided by writers such as Epstein and Louis Delluc were of natural features such as hills and trees, but this was certainly not a crucial factor. Rather the emphasis fell on photogénie being achieved through non-theatrical terms; assuming we are alive to cinema's capacity for revealing the energy and power in things we habitually take for granted, so their thinking went, drama is of secondary importance. Photogénie tells us that cinema's propensity is for showing us the world with a directness that precedes, or transcends, narrative, morality and aesthetic beauty. Whatever the relative merits or problems of such an account, the ability of film to grant a kind of prominence or agency to the non-human constituents of a textual world is certainly a recurring concern in this period.

However, an alternative current sought to celebrate and articulate not the medium's deep relationship with the material world, but rather its distinctiveness from that world. Hugo Münsterberg, an eminent psychologist fascinated with the nature of this emerging art, insisted on film's *freedom from* physical reality:

> The photoplay tells us the human story by overcoming the forms of the outer world, namely space, time, and causality, and by adjusting the events to the forms of the inner world, namely attention, memory, imagination, and emotion. (2002: 129)

Here, we find an early iteration of what would later be understood as formalist film theory, a tradition which focuses not on cinema's contract with physical reality, but on its potential for manipulating and reforming that reality into a self-enclosed work.

Sergei Eisenstein, perhaps the most influential theorist of film's first fifty years, was dissatisfied with the notion that the filmed world is, in itself, an important aesthetic or philosophical phenomenon. For Eisenstein (and other Soviet writers), meaning was not to be found in images so much as between them, in the act of editing. At times, Eisenstein's writing is so rigorously focused on what we might call the mechanics of montage – camera angles, graphic design, the strategic deployment of visual stimuli – that one could be forgiven for assuming that this would come at the cost of sensitive attention to the profilmic world (an assumption perhaps compounded by the tendency to place Eisenstein's ideas in opposition to those of André Bazin – see below). It would be more accurate to say that Eisenstein imagined cinema – and art more generally – as a site of productive conflict between nature and imagination, 'between organic inertia and creative tendency' (1949: 46), though one might be tempted to ask whether 'organic inertia' is an oxymoron. His later writings in particular show Eisenstein making room in his theorising for a film's environmental dynamics.

In *Nonindifferent Nature* (1987), first published in 1964, Eisenstein develops a complex account of how landscape provides films with what he calls a musical element. It was not uncommon in the early twentieth century to characterise natural landscape as a kind of transformative ingredient in film images – Ricciotto Canudo's 'Reflections on the Seventh Art' applauds Swedish cinema for introducing the 'ideal counterpoint' of the natural elements (1993: 292)– but Eisenstein's writing is unusual for the fact that he develops such ideas in a formalist manner. In other words, nature is not a subject to be revealed or redeemed by photographic representation, but rather a condition to which film form should aspire, through its crafting of an 'organic' structure:

> It is obvious that a work of this type has a very particular effect on the perceiver, not only because it is raised to the same level as natural phenomena but also because the law of its structuring is also the law governing those who perceive the work, for they too are part of organic nature. The perceiver feels organically tied, merged, and united with a work of this type, just as he feels himself one with and merged with the organic environment and nature surrounding him. (1987: 12)

Eisenstein's late writing is often difficult to interpret or to apply to other work, and his seemingly unquestioning belief in the wholeness and stability of organic structure has not dated especially well. But his basic position – namely that images of nature can be used strategically for the achievement of particular formal effects – is a useful counterpoint to the more pervasive idea of cinema as a realistic communicator of the natural world.

As mentioned, Eisenstein's formalist approach to the medium is often contrasted with André Bazin's championing of cinematic realism; Bazin himself identified the distinction between 'those who put their faith in the image and those who put their faith in reality' (1967: 24). There are many reasons to suppose that this second school of thinking is more temperamentally attuned to environmental particulars and complexities in film. Reviewing the position of Bazin and Siegfried Kracauer (another important theorist of film realism), V. F. Perkins paraphrased their general position in the following terms: 'a sonnet or a sonata created *a* world which might reflect the subjective vision of its maker; film recorded *the* world which existed objectively' (1972: 29). It would be very misleading to suggest that such writers thought of the world in primarily environmental or ecological terms, and Bazin's work in particular has strong social and religious impulses which have little to do with what we have come to understand as environmentalism. However, by suggesting that film as a medium offers us unequalled opportunities for 'passing through the continuum of physical existence' (Kracauer 1960: 64), realist writers remind us that cinema's recording function tends to allow for a more horizontal or mutually informing relationship between the human and the non-human world, when compared to literature and painting.

Here, for example, is Bazin on Roberto Rossellini's *Paisan* (1946):

> In the admirable final episode of the partisans surrounded in the marshlands, the muddy waters of the Po Delta, the reeds stretching away to the horizon, just sufficiently tall to hide the man crouching down in the little flat-bottomed boat, the lapping of the waves against the wood, all occupy a place of equal importance with the men. This dramatic role played by the marsh is due in great measure to deliberately intended qualities in the photography. This is why the horizon is always at the same height. Maintaining the same proportions between water and sky in every shot brings out one of the basic characteristics of this landscape. It is the exact equivalent, under conditions imposed by the screen, of the inner feeling men experience who are living between the sky and the water and whose lives are at the mercy of an infinitesimal shift of angle in relation to the horizon. (1971: 37)

Bazin admired Rossellini enormously, but he is not here crediting the director with having designed or consciously orchestrated the reeds or the lapping waves. Rather, he is crediting Rossellini with *allowing* cinema to 'bring out' natural phenomena which existed in reality, and now exist meaningfully in the film. Such sequences were valuable to Bazin because they exemplified how the 'conditions imposed by the screen' could be extraordinarily inclusive. As the passage above demonstrates, this theorising was still carried out in distinctly humanistic terms; Bazin's judgement ultimately returns to the question of human perception and human experience, but it is nevertheless an expanded experience, and one which is simply unintelligible without reference to the natural world. 'Cinema, he felt, allows us to examine the world without interiorizing it' (Andrew 1978: 114).

Fig. 1: Characteristics
of the landscape:
Paisan (1946)

This ability to examine the world at one remove, as it were, was a vital quality of cinema for Bazin, and was the result of the medium's mechanical character, what he called 'the instrumentality of a nonliving agent. For the first time an image of the world is formed automatically, without the creative intervention of man' (1967: 13). Developments in digital technology have complicated claims such as this, introducing myriad 'creative interventions' which would seem to disrupt Bazin's claim for cinema as a kind of disinterested witness of the world. But this sea change in film technology is by no means an abandonment or betrayal of the medium's potential for communicating the natural world. Yes, the language surrounding digital capabilities emphasises manipulation and simulation, and cinema can perhaps no longer lay claim to a particularly non-anthropocentric vision, at least not on the grounds for which it did throughout many decades. (It is interesting to reflect on what claims Bazin would make of the sequence in *Paisan* had Rossellini digitally inserted its reeds and lapping waves.) But it would be a mistake to dwell too long on certain ontological properties, however fundamental they have been for some theorists, and lose sight of all those other qualities and techniques at cinema's disposal – such as movement in time, sound/image combinations and flexibility of scale. As it turned away from photo-based indexicality, the medium by no means became less able to register and imagine environmental details and experiences.

In *Supercinema* (2013), William Brown argues the case for digital cinema's tendency towards non-anthropocentric models and visions. Because it doesn't give the impression of a world viewed from a single position, as analogue cinema has tended to, digital filmmaking is able to unbalance relations between 'figure' and 'ground' (to borrow terms normally applied to landscape painting). Watching digital cinema, Brown suggests, 'we can at times neither distinguish between nor separate space from that which fills it' (2013: 53); such technology helps us to 'understand that we only exist in relation with the world' (2013: 154).

Although she makes less bold claims for the philosophical and ethical value of digital film, Kristen Whissel (2014) focuses on certain CGI motifs, or 'emblems', and finds in them a capacity for filming the world in new ways. One of these emblems is verticality, the opening up of a severely underexplored dimension. 'Before the digital effects advances of the late 1980s and early 1990s,' writes Whissel, 'cinematic being-in-the-world remained, for the most part, anchored on the terrestrial plane of existence' (2014: 13), but recent developments have allowed filmmakers to engage different dimensions and trajectories. She takes as an example *Wo hu cang long* (*Crouching Tiger, Hidden Dragon*, 2000), and describes the range and complexity of physical action amongst tall trees as a genuinely novel opportunity for the medium. Such moments are not necessarily typical of digital practices, but then neither was Jean Vigo's *L'Atalante* (1934) or Roberto Rossellini's *Paisan* or Terrence Malick's *The New World* (2005) typical of photographic film. Like *Crouching Tiger, Hidden Dragon*, each of these used film technologies and qualities to document *and* to imagine meetings between people and their environments.

As writers on digital cinema often argue, worrying over the relative artificiality of a film's constitutive technology is invariably a fruitless and short-sighted task, simplifying as it does the 'frequently hybrid nature of indexicality' in both pre-digital and digital filmmaking (Purse 2013: 5). Film theory can help remind us of the medium's particular capacity for documenting and representing the natural environment, but this is best accompanied by a recognition of an individual film's meaningful details, as well as an awareness of the film-historical conditions out of which that film arose.

Film history

Rather than privileging a particular property of film as a medium (theory), or focusing in detail on exemplary works of film art (criticism), the discipline of film history tends to weave together industrial, aesthetic, technological and sociocultural factors, formulating questions about why something happened – or appeared – the way in which it did. That 'something' could be all manner of things; a film review, a portable sound recorder, a cycle of popular disaster films, the career of a costume designer. Alternatively, film can be understood and interrogated as a *document of* history (evidence of social norms and expectations), as much as a subject of history in its own right (images and materials worthy of reflective reconstruction and investigation). Most commonly, the discipline of film history develops a combination of the two. As Francesco Casetti writes, 'film was not only the perfect translator of the last century but also an active agent determining how its turbulent decades would unfold' (2008: 2).

Because nature is so often thought of as a constant, eternal backdrop against which historical fluctuations take place, and because cinema's lifespan has covered a period in which key historical dynamics are seen as moves 'away from nature' (communication technology, urbanisation, mass-media entertainment, industrial-scale agriculture), environmental questions have gathered little momentum in studies of film history. Landscape has perhaps been the main conceptual toolkit for those looking to historicise environmental dynamics in film; far-reaching images of the natural world, from *Stagecoach* (1939) to *Takhte siah* (*Blackboards*, 2000), can be validly interpreted as historically specific environmental representations. Such readings are often enabled by the fact that many cultures have traditions of landscape representation stretching back beyond cinema, to precedents in painting and literature (French impressionist painting, for example, has been exhaustively studied as an historically determined environmental vision). When we watch a Chinese film such as *Huang tudi* (*Yellow Earth*, 1984) or *Sanxia haoren* (*Still Life*, 2006), it may seem clear that these films' striking treatment of landscape is something embedded in far-reaching debates and traditions – about art history, national history and natural history. But it is nevertheless important to remain alive to the details of the films' own distinctive methods, such as the simple fact that, in the opening moments of *Yellow Earth*, the sound of wind precedes the appearance of the eponymous earth. As Helen Hok-Sze Leung notes, the combination of this sound with a folk tune creates a very specific rhetorical effect, a point of departure for subsequent images of vast, desolate terrain – and an influencing factor in *how* we interpret those images (2003: 192).

Sometimes, it is necessary to consider very specific and localised circumstances which have shaped a film's environmental content; not just broad traditions and cultures, but particular regions or events or individuals. For example, Andrei Tarkovsky's *Stalker* (1979) was released seven years before the Chernobyl nuclear disaster in the Soviet Union, and that film's extraordinary vision of a depopulated but eerily animate 'zone' has had a considerable influence on how the real-life 'zone of alienation' surrounding the power plant is understood and represented – right up to the video game *S.T.A.L.K.E.R.: Shadow of Chernobyl* (GSC, 2007). Films as diverse as *Zemlya* (*Earth*, 1930), *The Texas Chainsaw Massacre* (1974) and *Loong Boonmee raleuk chat* (*Uncle Boonmee Who Can Recall His Past Lives*, 2010) similarly invite studies that situate their treatment of the natural environment in specific socio-historical contexts, and in relation to con-temporaneous thinking on wilderness, wildness, stewardship, material consumption, technology, biology and ethics.

Film history, of course, does not necessarily take an individual film as its starting point. Sometimes, an environmental approach can be taken to the study of industrial trends or filmmaking technologies. Nicole Starosielski's writing on 'underwater cinema', for example, explores how the early twen-tieth-century films of John Ernest Williamson, such as *Thirty Leagues Under the Sea* (1914), were enabled by naval technology, and Starosielski argues that submarine filming throughout film history has tended to involve the sharing of resources and footage, because of the sheer 'strenuousness and precariousness of production in underwater environments' (2013: 151). Here and elsewhere in environmental histories of film, physical diffi-culty and logistical effort become important parts of the historical account. A guiding question might be phrased as: What labour was necessary/ affordable/desirable in order for environmental details to have appeared as they do in a certain film or group of films? In *Hollywood Cinema and the Real Los Angeles*, Mark Shiel traces the financially motivated development in studio architecture away from glass and steel, and towards concrete – a shift which seriously compromised filmmakers' ability to incorporate natu-ral light (2012: 162). Film history is populated with many 'sub-plots' such as this, in which environmental spectacle and scope and fidelity can best be understood in relation to complex networks of economy and ambition.

A different approach would be to take as a case study a recognised 'chapter' of film history, and ask to what extent its coherence or its achievements have anything to do with environmental dynamics – whether these be understood in terms of production, reception, technology, narrative or aesthetics. In the same way that a feminist approach can challenge our understanding and evaluation of, for example, the French New Wave, so would an ecocritical approach challenge us to ask *what was going on in those films* with regard to the natural environment. Such an exercise would probably not completely overhaul the conventional narrative of that period; Bazinian realism, cinephilia and modernist reflexivity would remain as defining features of the New Wave. But there is still scope to explore the episodes of pastoral parody in *Pierrot le Fou* (1965) and *Weekend* (1967) to ask what particular locations attracted New Wave filmmakers away from Paris, and to reflect on why Antoine Doinel finds himself at the beach (of all places), frozen in time, at the end of *Les quatre cent coups* (*The 400 Blows*, 1959).

This famous climactic image is taken up by Lúcia Nagib in *World Cinema and the Ethics of Realism* (2011), and connected to other moments in film history which Nagib sees as similarly charged with aesthetic-revolutionary purpose. She identifies a trans-historical – but still historically informed – tradition of 'physical cinema', in which bold and original films demonstrate their ambition through an unusually intense engagement (in the form of running) with the profilmic landscape:

> Performed in reality, in vast wintry landscapes, burning deserts or Arctic sea ice, these races invariably take the upper hand over the diegesis and impose their own narrative, one related to the characters' recognizing, experiencing, demarcating and taking possession of a territory, and, in doing so, taking possession of a people and its culture. (2011: 12)

To think about film history environmentally does not necessarily require a rigorous focus on a specific region, culture, period or ecosystem. Tracing motifs or narrative details across geographical and historical boundaries can be similarly revealing.

Andrew Higson combines a number of the historical approaches discussed here in his influential article about British realist cinema of the late 1950s and early 1960s, 'Space, Place, Spectacle: Landscape and Townscape in the "Kitchen Sink" Film' (1984). Like Nagib, he takes as his starting point a certain gesture or motif that seems to reappear in a number of films (in this case, a long shot of an industrial town from a nearby hill), but Higson's examples are from a historically coherent and popularly known cycle of films, namely British 'kitchen sink' realist dramas, such as *Saturday Night and Sunday Morning* (1960) and *A Taste of Honey* (1961) (albeit with selected references back to documentary films of the 1930s and 1940s). As a film historian, Higson is particularly interested in the relationship between the visual cliché of the long shot and the critical discourse surrounding the films, much of which was based on claims for a kind of realist integrity.

Higson's essay is not focused on environmental ethics or aesthetics as such, but it asks how a film's way of looking at the physical world can be embedded in a particular cultural and critical context – an instructive approach for environmental film studies. The discussion begins by positing a distinction between (narrative) space and (real, historical) place, suggesting that the convention of the landscape or townscape shot exposes a tension within the films between storytelling and realist ambitions. Higson tries to communicate quite how hackneyed the convention is by way of a persistent use of capitals – The Long Shot of That Town from That Hill – and suggests that such images cannot help but function as visually pleasurable spectacle, corrupting the film's realist credentials. The belief that landscape images (in and beyond cinema) impair narrative, and that they may even carry with them a reactionary political undertow, is quite a popular one among art historians and political geographers. What marks out Higson's work here is the particular contradictions he identifies in the 'kitchen sink' films between what he calls 'moral realism' and 'the sympathetic gaze of the bourgeoisie' (1984: 4, 17). He writes of how 'the real historical landscape, local and concrete, legitimates and authenticates' the films' moral impulses (1984: 5); it is as if the films want to be true to the particularity of a given physical environment, whilst also striving for some kind of transcendence. The pull between mimetic specificity and far-reaching allegory is a consistent theme in studies of nature on film, and Higson successfully identifies a very historically precise articulation of that tension.

The challenge of reconciling geography and storytelling is another of the chief concerns on display in 'Space, Place, Spectacle' (and is a theme we shall return to in Chapter 2). For example, Higson recounts a moment in *Saturday Night and Sunday Morning* in which two characters meet at the castle which overlooks Nottingham. The moment is perfectly plausible in terms of narrative, but is also a rather conspicuous display, on the part of the film, of the city; the overt references to this spectacle in the film's dialogue (one character chides the other one for dreamily admiring the view) are, according to Higson, attempts by the film to reintegrate the environment into the narrative. While *Saturday Night and Sunday Morning* may or may not hold our interest as a dramatic film, it is, according to Higson, vividly indicative of a moment in British film history in which films were supposed to have been closely tied to certain, real, physical places: 'The machinery of criticism, promotion and selling, and the dominant historical memory of these films, endlessly stresses the detail of location, but this detail is a product of moral demands rather than structural (narrative) demands' (1984: 8).

In these terms there is a trade-off between geographical validity and formal fluency, and one which Higson acknowledges was unlikely to satisfy those critics (a relatively small group in the Britain of 1962) who were much more interested in the aesthetic than the social project of a film, critics more concerned that 'the problem of the relationship between character and environment be worked through at the level of narrative and mise-en-scène (1984: 16). Higson quotes a particularly damning survey of 'kitchen sink' filmmaking, published in *Movie* and written by V. F. Perkins, who would go on to profoundly influence a great many writers of long-form, sustained film criticism – work focused on a film's expressive achievements, and not its realist or sociological credentials. What would this alternative approach look for, and find, in a film's environmental subjects and meanings?

Film criticism

While film theory reaches towards arguments and insights that are potentially applicable to the medium at large, film criticism instead takes an individual film (or a select group of films) as its subject matter. Film criticism rarely attends very closely or imaginatively to non-human environments; evaluations of performance and narrative interest tend to dominate such writing, and if natural environments attract attention, it will often be either as plot details or items of spectacle. But Alex Clayton and Andrew Klevan write that the best criticism '*deepens* our interest in individual films, *reveals* new meanings and perspectives, *expands* our sense of the medium, *confronts* our assumptions about value, and *sharpens* our capacity to discriminate' (2011: 1), and a sensitivity to a filmed environment is often a hallmark of such work. A work of film criticism is unlikely to begin by asking whether *Titanic* is a film about nature. But it might well find, through a sustained engagement with that film's design and development, with its most compelling and fully achieved sequences, that nature does indeed *matter* to that film. As Clayton and Klevan's terms suggest, it is not the case that criticism lacks the ambition or reach of theory, but rather that it is more methodologically inclined to allow films themselves to actively influence the terms of our interpretation and analysis.

A number of the most important and influential writers in the tradition of film criticism have, at one time or another, found themselves engaging with work that requires some sort of 'environmental orientation'. It is perhaps not surprising that the expansion referred to by Clayton and Klevan often involves a revitalised awareness of the non-human world – what Christian Keathley, paraphrasing Bazin, calls the 'festival of concrete details' (2006: 69). Sometimes this can take the form of a fleeting, intensified attention to seemingly incidental details in the filmed environment, such as moving clouds or intensely coloured flora, and this is often a feature of so-called cinephilic film criticism. For example, when Kent Jones, in his remarkable study of *L'Argent* (1983), describes one particular transition as a 'sudden – and altogether shocking – entry of greenery, earth and air into the momentum' of the work (1999: 76), no claim is being for the film's environmental character at large. But the author's responsiveness to the fullness of the story world is vital to his understanding of its meaning, and to his judgement of the director's priorities and distinctiveness; of a later sequence, Jones writes: 'The lyricism of nature, the leaves in the trees – an old gig in cinema, usually overlit, overly precious. Bresson films it with such delicacy that it might be the first time you've ever seen it in a film' (1999: 83).

Stanley Cavell, a philosopher who has been an influential figure in long-form film criticism, does something slightly different with his observation of a moonlit stream 'shattered by stars' (2005: 137) in a brief sequence of Frank Capra's romantic comedy, *It Happened One Night* (1934). Here, Cavell connects this moment to a brief exchange of dialogue which takes place the following day, during which Peter Warne (Clark Gable) dreamily describes 'those nights when you and the moon and the water all become one'. As Cavell notes, these words in themselves have little aesthetic or philosophical interest, but when placed in the context of the film's images (and when we recall the important and somewhat mysterious fact that Warne did not seem to consciously register the beauty of the previous night's setting), the moment takes on an intensified complexity, enabling Cavell to situate the film in Shakespearean and American transcendental traditions. The stream, and the reverie it seems to prompt, does not have a major bearing on Cavell's interpretation of *It Happened One Night*, but the passage in question is still an excellent example of how an open and generous critical reading will often find that a film's world is not limited to human drama. (It is also an important reminder that telling features of a film's environmentality can be found in dialogue.)

At other times, such observations are more fully built in to a developed and sustained interpretation. 'Sunny Skies', Shigehiko Hasumi's celebrated article on weather (and conversations about weather) in the films of Yasujirō Ozu, finds that, with 'an almost cruel consistency, Ozu ignores the seasons' (1997: 120). For a writer who knows the work of Ozu extensively and intimately, and one who is also familiar with Japanese weather, the curious inertia of atmospheric conditions (why no rain?) in films such as *Banshun* (*Late Spring*, 1949) and *Tokyo Monogatari* (*Tokyo Story*, 1953) becomes an important part of the films' aesthetic deliberateness. The relentless sunlight in Ozu's films is, for Shigehiko, evidence of

Fig. 2: A moonlit stream 'shattered by stars': *It Happened One Night* (1934)

his departure from Japanese aesthetic ideals, and helps to explain the unusual and deeply affecting 'excess of clarity' in his films (1997: 121).

Addressed as it is to a filmmaker's body of work, 'Sunny Skies' could be classified as a work of auteurist criticism. Studying a director's priorities and techniques across a range of films is one way to appreciate that the presence and distinctiveness of environmental details in cinema is not inevitable or incidental, and that it can be closely tied to a filmmaker's vision. Sometimes this takes the form of a director's persistent interest in a particular element (for example, water in the films of Lucretia Martel), a particular location (beaches in the films of Eric Rohmer), a particular technique (Terrence Malick's travelling Steadicam shots), or a particular genre (the road movies of Wim Wenders). Daniel Morgan's writing on the later films of Jean-Luc Godard is a rare case of auteurist criticism in which the filmmaker in question overtly engages, through his or her work, in theoretically informed debates about nature and perception (2013: 69–119). As Morgan explores in considerable detail, Godard became interested in nature as a type of iconography, rather than a pure or pre-intellectualised subject. His shots of landscapes and seascapes are not, according to Morgan, affective windows on the world, but pointers to a lineage of philosophical and cultural references, from Lucretius and Schiller to Marx and Shakespeare.

It is by no means the case that every director's oeuvre can be fruitfully explored in ecocritical terms. The films of Kathryn Bigelow, Terence Davis, John Woo and Jacques Tati, for example, would not necessarily repay close attention to environmental conditions of the kind explored in this book. But those, it would seem, are exceptional cases. Hungarian film critic Yvette Bíró wrote that the 'dialogue between man and world is uninterruptable' (2008: 19), and the vast majority of celebrated filmmakers continue that dialogue by engaging – to a greater or lesser extent – with the rhythms, materials and connotations of the natural world.

'"Cocoon of Fire"': Awakening to Love in Murnau's *Sunrise*' (2012), an article by George Toles published in *Film International*, is an excellent example of how imaginative and precise interpretation can deepen our understanding of a film's creative treatment of nature. *Sunrise: A Song of Two Humans* (1927) is one of the most celebrated of all silent features, and is often understood as a particularly successful marriage of American melodrama and German Expressionism. Toles is more than aware of the film's important industrial and film-historical context, but focuses his own analysis on questions of structure and temporality. More specifically, he claims that viewers of *Sunrise* 'feel the rhythmic balance of night and day as a deep mystery which the still new medium of motion pictures is able and eager to explore', and something which persists 'with or without synchronized human accompaniment' (2012: 9). The idea of 'synchronisation' is a useful one, reminding us of how human drama, when filmed, can be set against contrasting or complementary natural processes. Many films make some attempt to connect their narrative structures to seasonal cycles – perhaps none more diligently than *Bom yeoreum gaeul gyeoul geurigo bom* (*Spring, Summer, Fall, Winter… and Spring*, 2003) – but Toles finds in *Sunrise* something other than a straightforward alignment between action and environment.

This is partly achieved by him discovering how fully and seriously Murnau seems to regard the idea of spiritual and emotional awakening, as encapsulated in the metaphor of a loving woman's face as a rising sun. Ecocritical writing on film and fiction often treats with (justifiable) caution the offhand way in which some creative artists indulge in pathetic fallacy, or what Toles describes as 'the unseemly, primitive obtrusiveness of literal correspondences' (2012: 10) between emotional currents and worldly phenomena; such moments are even more likely to be deemed problematic when the convention links a forgiving wife with the ever-dependable and life-giving sun. But Toles convincingly argues that Murnau has integrated this image-idea so completely into *Sunrise* ('all the images of Murnau's film are wondrously coordinated with this endpoint' (2012: 13)), that the film transcends facile Romanticism.

This reading is enabled by the fact that Toles is not seeking in *Sunrise* a biocentric view of the world, nor one governed by the ambitions of realism. Human experience remains at the centre of this interpretation, but it is what might be thought of as an expanded, situated humanism: 'We must participate in the dawn […] for the dawn to be made real. Each day's experiential task is to unlearn as fully as possible what we think we know so we will be in a position to reimagine it' (2012: 14). The almost euphoric tone here is buttressed by a historical discussion of Murnau's changing relationship with Expressionism, a mode which conventionally emphasised the painful discontinuities between individuals and their world. Toles shows that, in *Sunrise*, Murnau seems to have inverted the logic of Expressionism, transforming his vision of human experience 'from private chaos to an unforced attunement with natural process' (2012: 16). As a work of criticism, his essay thus establishes a very interesting framework through which to understand the pressing significance of the natural world in *Sunrise*; but this would only get us so far were it not accompanied by a detailed treatment of the film's images and sounds (this 'silent film' has a synchronised score).

There are many points at which Toles' careful attention to the film's textual details fulfils this promise. For example, he observes that, during a brief chase sequence through forest terrain, Murnau chooses *not* to visually emphasise the potentially intimidating environment. He also draws our attention to a moment at which the film's reunited lovers see before them, in a shared vision of happiness, images of a bright and sunny meadow. For Toles, Murnau is fully aware that this glimpse of 'dimestore picturesque' is a 'touchingly insufficient container for the depth of feeling they have arrived at' (2012: 25); Murnau's own environmental imagination is thus delicately distinguished from that of his protagonists, and indeed the gap separating those two worldviews is crucial to the film's power.

Throughout, Toles demonstrates how film criticism can help us understand a film's environmental poetics as something shaped by and answerable to its other dramatic and expressive elements. Watching and listening to the non-human world in *Sunrise* is, for Toles, a means towards a better understanding of the film. And if this kind of account can along the way

Fig. 3: The 'dimestore picturesque' shared by husband and wife: *Sunrise: A Song of Two Humans* (1927)

give rise to useful observations about German and American film history, and the broader capacities of cinema, so much the better. But the lasting impression of this essay is of someone who has reached the climax of *Sunrise* and has found no other way of doing justice to its profundity than to describe its world in as full a form as possible; sound, image, narrative, bodies, elements, atmosphere:

> Late in *Sunrise*, the farmer leans forward in one of the lantern-lit nocturnal rescue boats sent out to find his missing wife, and he repeatedly calls out her name. His voice is replaced by a French horn, and the watery surfaces in their soft, vagrant, rippling mirror state seem to attend to the lament and form nebulous images in reply. The bulrushes, to be sure, randomly carry the loosely bound body of the unconscious wife forward in the slow current. She cannot hear the calling voice and the lake is as impersonal in its renewed calm as it was in its previous storm fury. Nevertheless, the fact that the searching husband's voice is musical (not limited to a human's desperate call) links without strain the husband's needs with the separate (but not entirely separate) music of the becalmed lake. The moonlit surface of the water does not register his agitation; it cannot care whether the body it carries stays afloat or sinks. But the water's own rhythm in the vast night is somehow in accord with everything that rests upon it, that floats or sails in its element. The sky, the boats on their rescue mission, the light from various sources, the distant shore, are all dreamy collaborators 'facing each other', as it were, while making their separate arrangements. They make a common music in the midst of missed and fugitive connections. All that comes into view in the water, every sound that the music conjures for our imaginations in the flickering darkness, can be taken as a reply to the man's act of searching. He does not immediately discover what he seeks but the lake is not merely forsaking him to his own anxious mood, or mocking him by refusing to partake of that mood, or positing 'emptiness' in the act of withholding. Just as the community joins him in his effort to retrieve his lost spouse from the lake (however dim the prospect of success), the lake too 'joins up' with him. It is not only where he is; for a time it becomes who he is. What can we say about the farmer now? He

is a man in a boat holding a lantern, given over entirely to looking at the water for signs. His past does not supply residual definition, a residual something to fall back on or to carry us beyond the search's end. He is wholly the incomplete being struggling to see anything that might confirm his hope of lingering life (his own and his wife's) in the mist-shrouded ebb and flow. His fate seems overwhelmingly tied to what the lake, for good or ill, brings to light. He belongs, as much as a medieval knight to his quest, to the act of pursuing the watery trail. (2012: 16)

2 FILM NARRATIVE AND THE NATURAL ENVIRONMENT

Chapter 1 outlined how an environmental perspective can contribute to and complement some key methods of film study. This necessarily encompassed questions of theory, history, style, technology, authorship, ideology and narrative. Partly because it is such a vital framework for most people's conscious and sub-conscious engagement with films, and partly because it is often thought of as a quintessentially human capacity, narrative requires further consideration. This chapter will ask what it means to recognise the natural environment not just as an ingredient of a film's story world, but as an important part of its storytelling technique.

Narrative and nature

A narrative is a deliberately ordered series of causally linked events, each one happening in space and time. Depending on the medium in question, both an author and a narrator can have a determining influence on what we understand of that space and time. And human characters within a narrative will respond to and act upon their spatial and temporal constraints. Even when we begin with this relatively straightforward description of narrative, there are already a number of ways that the natural environment could be said to play a part:

1. The space in which the narrative events happen is, to a greater or lesser extent, a natural space, understood as relatively untouched by human design – such as the forest in a fairy tale. This is what is normally meant by a natural 'setting'.
2. The actions and attitudes of characters are, to a greater or lesser extent, motivated by environmental features and processes – such as the scaling of a mountain, or the onset of a drought.
3. The author and/or narrator creatively emphasises certain aspects or properties of the natural environment – such as when a playwright specifies that a scene take place at sunset, or when a film's soundtrack stresses the presence of nearby wildlife.

It should be clear that, in any engaging and sophisticated narrative, these are deeply connected to one another.

For example, a famous and distressing scene in Shakespeare's *King Lear* begins with Lear shouting at the powerful storm in which he is engulfed: 'Blow, winds, and crack your cheeks! rage! blow!' (3.2.1). A windswept heath is the setting for the action, but these conditions also *dictate* the action to a large extent, compounding Lear's distress and prompting him (along with the Fool and Kent) to retreat to a shelter at the scene's end. Shakespeare's language, meanwhile, does not just present us with a generic 'storm'; we are reminded, through the consciousness of Lear, that the storm is a compendium of different elemental forces – 'Sulphurous and Thought-executing Fires' (3.2.4); 'all-shaking Thunder' (3.2.5) – and that such tumultuous natural processes can leave us confused about the relationship between man and world. Lear early on seems to recognise, and perhaps even take solace in, the absolute indifference of the storm to his personal troubles, but at a later moment cannot resist the temptation of seeing the environment as a collaborator with his own daughters against him. The heath and the storm (do we distinguish between the two?) can be seen as basic ingredients of this scene, its fundamental coordinates, but Shakespeare obviously takes these and capitalises on their dramatic and expressive potential. Setting is one thing, an important consideration in studies of narrative; the aesthetic treatment of that setting, the means by which it becomes part of meaningful narration, is altogether more complex. A brief summary of *King Lear* could tell us that a key scene is set in a fierce storm on exposed terrain, but much closer study is needed if we are to properly understand how and why that storm becomes a 'horrible Pleasure' for the play's main character (3.2.19).

Unless we define these terms very broadly, *King Lear* does not offer us evidence or documentation of a natural environment, but rather provocative thoughts about our relationship to that environment. Film, as we have seen in the writing of some early theorists, has the potential to document *and* narrate simultaneously, and this is one of its most distinctive characteristics as a medium. But before venturing into specific film stories and their environmental characteristics, it is useful to consider the ways in which far-reaching and culturally influential narrative blueprints – myths, genres and modes – have their own built-in tendencies for 'managing' the natural world in particular ways.

A good example of this is the utopian mode, which encompasses a great many individual narrative works, the majority which will share certain basic presumptions about nature – its plenty, but also its importance as a human resource. (In so-called 'ecotopian' narrative, such presumptions are brought to the forefront of the work.) Greg Garrard's introductory book, *Ecocriticism* (2004) suggests four other modes or large-scale metaphors which tend to form the basis of cultural reflections on the environment: pastoral, wilderness, apocalypse and dwelling. Each of these has a complex lineage and contains many sub-varieties and contradictions, but they all warrant our attention as very basic and pervasive visions of the environment; as a beautiful place to which we can flee (pastoral), as an untamed and uncivilised force (wilderness), a perpetually looming catastrophe (apocalypse), and as an achieved harmony between the social and the ecological (dwelling). These foundational ideas are built upon, populated and illustrated by storytellers and artists – sometimes more creatively than others. Most of us would be able to recall novels and films and plays and songs and paintings which answer to these rough characterisations.

Reflecting on these structural patterns helps us remember just quite how formulaic cultural representations tend to be in their narrative renderings of nature. But such an approach is also in danger of obscuring our sense of the variety *within* a particular mode; to dwell on 'grand narratives' of environmental representation might mean we miss the ways in which narrative artists selectively emphasise certain natural features and forces for certain creative ends. Take, for example, the narrative role played by particular natural elements. Earth, wind, fire and water do not have fixed sets of associations or meanings, but each one *does* have distinctive material qualities which lend it certain narrative potential. Water, for example, is reflective, and so is more likely to invoke or accompany moments of contemplation than, for example, wind. We tend to imagine earth and stone as the taken-for-granted underpinnings of our comings and goings; fire, meanwhile, is more likely to speak to us of disruption and chaos. Add to these examples the range of plants, animals and geographic features on which a storyteller might draw, and it soon becomes clear how a narrative's environmental character should be understood not just in terms of its genre or mode, but how that mode is 'fleshed out' with details.

Film narrative and nature

As we move towards the case of environmental storytelling in cinema, a very useful starting point is the work of Charles and Mirella Jona Affron in *Sets in Motion: Art Direction and Film Narrative* (1995). The book offers a framework for the interpretation and analysis of set design in film, and although the authors focus almost entirely on deliberately designed and constructed sets (rather than found locations), their terms are pertinent for a much wider variety of work. In summary, Affron and Affron suggest that the narrative role of set design can be understood on a five-point scale, running from transparency to opacity: set as denotation (simply establishing time and place); set as punctuation (making occasional claims on the attention of audiences); set as embellishment (narratively and rhetorically prominent); set as artifice (mannered, defamiliarising décor) and set as narrative (single-locale films). This is a very productive guide for thinking about the variety of relationships which can emerge in a film between story and space, particularly a film conceived for and shot in studio conditions. Similar claims can be made about the use of natural environments in film; for example, the 'punctuative' role of the hunting grounds in *La règle du jeu* (*Rules of the Game*, 1939), or the 'embellishing' role of many outdoor spaces in *Brokeback Mountain* (2005).

But it is important to note those ways in which the Affrons' model does not quite translate to natural environments, points at which the application breaks down. The specific sets which feature as many of the examples in *Sets in Motion* (offices, bedrooms, staircases) can normally be understood as relatively isolated elements, whereas environmental features are more likely to 'bleed' from one scene or sequence to another. The opacity which is attributed to some sets, in which 'design is rendered specific and legible through the invention of the patently unreal' (1995: 39), is difficult to transpose to natural features; would the materials themselves be visibly artificial (an effect used in *Zabriskie Point* (1970)), or would the attention awarded to them in the film be deliberately excessive or baroque (a claim we could make of *Barry Lyndon* (1975))? But perhaps most significantly, there is the simple fact that as viewers of *Brokeback Mountain* and *Barry Lyndon*, *Staroye i novoye* (*The General Line*, 1929) and *Daughters of the Dust* (1993), we tend to believe that the physical environments on screen are not created by artists, however carefully they have been woven into a story's design.

Of all the narrative arts, film is perhaps the best able to retain some sense of a world beyond the control of the artist(s) involved. Joseph Conrad's Congo River or Willa Cather's Great Plains are undeniably charged by their connections to actual environments, but the Amazon basin in Werner Herzog's *Fitzcarraldo* (1982) or the Zagros mountains in Samira Makhmalbaf's *Blackboards* (2000) have an altogether different level of independence and specificity. We may know that such environments only appear to us by way of selective cinematography and editing, but there is nevertheless a sense with film that physical places are non-negotiable pre-requisites for narrative action – more than points of reference or vivid embellishments. Whether or not the film's action is ostensibly set in a real-world place (the Peruvian Amazon, the Iranian borderlands), and whether or not this specificity really matters, a film story is visibly, audibly and inescapably *somewhere*.

In practice, we know that films often have us believe one place to be another (so-called 'Spaghetti Westerns' are a case in point). What we shall explore in this chapter, however, is not the veracity of films as documents of particular environments, but rather the ways in which a film's narrative emerges in part from its embeddedness in an environment. I will of course concentrate on those films where the non-human world accrues a special significance or intensity, and make no claims for this approach to film study being universally applicable; we would be unlikely to understand *Citizen Kane* (1941) and *Chung Hing sam lam* (*Chungking Express*, 1994) more fully, for example, if we forcibly interpreted them as environmental stories. But a great many film narratives do make considerable use of environmental qualities and associations, and it is important to reflect on some of the key terms we employ when discussing and interpreting these tendencies.

It is no surprise, for example, that many writers and viewers reach for the term 'landscape' when describing and interpreting filmed environments. Although it slips between referring to a place and to an image of that place, the word itself seems more precise than 'nature', and more responsive to the fact that film offers us framed images (rather than abstract ideas). It is also a word more adept than 'nature' at registering an intermingling of human and non-human qualities, and can be freely used to describe urban and non-urban sites. Crucially, 'landscape' does of course bring with it fine-art connotations, and so its use points to processes of looking and interpreting, of aesthetic interpretation. Nobody seriously thinks that 'nature' reaches us, in a film, unmediated – and landscape as an idea successfully acknowledges the impurities of representation. As W. J. T. Mitchell writes of landscape painting, it is best understood as a 'representation of something that is already a representation in its own right' (2002: 14).

But landscape can also be said to sit rather uncomfortably with our understanding (and expectations) of film narrative. This is the premise of a very useful and much-cited essay by Martin Lefebvre, 'Between Setting and Landscape in the Cinema' (2006). Setting, as Lefebvre explains, is a feature of virtually every imaginable narrative, whether or not it is specified or emphasised. Landscape, meanwhile, is a kind of 'anti-setting', a way of looking at the world that has nothing to do with temporal developments, complications or resolutions (the stuff of narrative); Lefebvre's key term here is 'space freed from eventhood' (2006: 22). He explains that cinema spectatorship often requires us to choose between spectacle and narrative (noting that classical conventions invariably promote the latter), and that to enter into a mode of landscape spectatorship is to automatically move out of narrative engagement. This is the point at which setting becomes landscape.

Take, for example, *Force Majeure* (2014). This film chronicles an unhappy skiing holiday, in which marital tensions come to the fore after a husband and father, Tomas (Johannes Kuhnke) prioritises his own safety during a mechanically controlled avalanche. He then refuses to acknowledge the fact that he momentarily abandoned his family, a refusal which sparks the growing resentment and incredulity of his wife, Ebba

(Lisa Loven Kongsli). It is a rigorously structured film, in which long and tense dialogue-heavy scenes are sometimes punctuated by 'landscape intermissions' – unpeopled long shots of the ski resort's mountainous surroundings (accompanied by a Vivaldi motif). To watch *Force Majeure* is to experience something very much in accordance with Lefebvre's model, as conventional staples of film narrative (changing human relationships filmed at relatively close quarters) invite one mode of audience engagement, while occasional interruptions prompt a switch to a kind of a-temporal landscape spectatorship.

However, and as Lefebvre is very much aware, interesting films are unlikely to recycle these distinctions uncritically, and the crucial scene in *Force Majeure* is a case in point. Tomas, Ebba and their two children are eating a meal together on the deck of the ski resort's restaurant; the scene is filmed in a single, static take, with the family and other diners in the middle distance, and the snowy mountains in the distance. When the controlled avalanche begins, Tomas tries to reassure his family that they have nothing to worry about, but the powerful drift does indeed reach the building, prompting considerable panic and fear. The danger is short-lived, though, and the family soon return to their table, shaken but physically unscathed. How do the terms of setting and landscape help us understand this short but striking sequence? Firstly, we should note that the surroundings are given no independent recognition through establishing shots or any other means; the mountains are very much a backdrop, and are initially treated as such by the characters (whose attention is at first focused on the food). And yet, we could actually characterise the camera's position as one set to a 'landscape mode'; it frames the mountains in a visually coherent and pleasing manner, and makes no adjustment or accommodation for the human characters and actions (even in the extreme shift from mundane table talk to mortal fear). The mountains constitute a setting inasmuch as they 'host' the narrative events (the leisurely meal, the threatening avalanche), but they also hold sway over those events, and of course become a narrative agent very quickly. It would be difficult to describe them as a *mere* setting, but neither is their visual power dependent on a lack of narrative context, a freedom from eventhood. They are not clearly a cinematic landscape either.

Tomas's first reaction to the avalanche is to film it on his phone, a recording which will resurface much later in the narrative. We may or may

Fig. 4: Landscape and narrative: *Force Majeure* (2014)

not choose to interpret this as a reflexive gesture; at the very least, it is a characterising gesture, contributing to our understanding of Tomas as a rather ineffective and opportunistic man, as well as a husband and father not terribly well attuned to the needs of his family. This leads us on to another important facet of environmentality in film narratives – how characters' own distinctive relationships with their natural surroundings inform our understanding (and evaluation) of them. Because ecocriticism as an approach has been understandably wary of readings which explore environmental qualities purely as tools for embellishing anthropocentric narratives, this is a relatively underexplored area, but the very particular manner with which a character looks at, moves in, controls, submits to, talks about – and even ignores – an environment can be very significant indeed. Karin (Ingrid Bergman) in *Stromboli* (1950), Ron (Rock Hudson) in *All That Heaven Allows* (1955), Mona (Sandrine Bonnaire) in *Sans toit ni loi* (*Vagabond*, 1985); these are people whose navigation of material surroundings is absolutely central to what we know and think of them.

The same is true of the characters at the heart of *The Wind* (1928), *Local Hero* (1983) and *La mujer sin cabeza* (*The Headless Woman*, 2008), explored in this chapter. As many readers will already know, very little connects these films by way of style and tone, ambition and execution, contexts and points of reference. I am of course keen to demonstrate the broad applicability of environmental approaches to film narrative (across periods, cultural traditions, genres, etc), but this choice of case studies is not wilfully random. I have chosen films which tend not to 'look at' environmental surroundings in the way we might associate with important landscape filmmakers, from John Ford and Andrei Tarkovsky to Patrick Keiller and Theo Angelopoulos. The non-human world becomes narratively interesting in these film not because we see it with unusual regularity or duration, but because it is woven into patterns of behaviour, action and perspective with what seems to me a special degree of care and imagination.

The Wind

Some film narratives are momentarily guided or complicated by environmental conditions; a ravine might prove to be an insurmountable barrier, for example, or a dense forest could offer temporary shelter and rejuvenation. These same conditions will invariably influence not only the patterns of action and causality (preventing or hastening a particular action, say), but also the less verifiable qualities of atmosphere, tone, association and expectation. So, for example, a forest setting is not only a material place with certain narrative affordances, but also a textual element which can trigger interpretive comparisons with fairy tales or Shakespearean comedy. It has both practical and associative implications for the narrative.

The Wind is a valuable case study for discussions of environmental narrative because it is so rich on both these counts; its story is directly built upon the immediate dangers and opportunities afforded by natural conditions, but the film is also very much about how those features are bound up with individual psychology and cultural behavior (most crucially regarding gender). The film tells the story of Letty (Lillian Gish), an orphan who travels from Virginia to Texas to stay with her cousin, and whose experience there is fundamentally shaped by the environment. The wind (which, of course, cannot be filmed as such) daunts, disturbs and threatens Letty, but her ordeal is not a personal or private experience; the manner in which the heroine responds to the unfamiliar climate very much governs her social interactions and, ultimately, her fate.

The natural environment is so overwhelmingly important in The Wind – from the introductory intertitle which tells of 'nature's vastness' and 'fierce elements', right through to the extraordinary final image of a married

Fig. 5: Hiding from the elements: *The Wind* (1928)

couple in defiant embrace on a windswept threshold – that this aspect of the film almost seems to leave no opportunity for developed commentary. But we shall focus on a particular aspect of the film's narrative, namely the extent to which qualities of the natural environment reach us (the audience) *through* an individual's consciousness.

Point of view, one of the key dynamics in any narrative, can take on a new kind of significance and complexity in narratives which privilege environmental conditions. In *Narration in Light: Studies in Cinematic Point of View*, George Wilson writes about viewers' 'epistemic distance' from a film, describing the implicit contract between film and audience which states that many common-sense assumptions will apply to a film world, but that some will not:

> a spectator who is to achieve even a rudimentary understanding of a segment of film narrative must draw nonstop upon the incredible diversity of perceptual knowledge that we ordinarily and untendentiously assume we have about actual things and processes. This knowledge includes, of course, our more trustworthy beliefs about the nature and operation of the extracinematic world. (1986: 4)

This common-sense basis on which narratives are built (and from which fantasy narratives depart more than realist narratives, for example) becomes a somewhat troubled notion with a film such as *The Wind*, because this is a work concerned with extraordinary and exceptional 'operations' of the world, namely extreme weather. The environmental characteristics of the diegesis (which in many films would constitute the 'nature' described by Wilson) are in *The Wind* relatively unfamiliar to most film viewers and – more importantly – are unfamiliar to the film's central character, Letty. As the film develops, the heroine becomes increasingly distressed by the environment, in concert with her increasing distress about her personal situation. And it becomes difficult to know whether to interpret the violent climate as a kind of poetic exteriorisation of Letty's psychological trauma or an indifferent and coincidental material phenomenon which compounds her trauma. Had Letty arrived in the region with a companion, or had the film begun with scenes of her elsewhere (back home in Virginia, described in one intertitle as 'thick with wild violets'), this effect would be lessened; we would have a firmer grasp on the relative objectivity of the film's environmental mise-en-scène. As it stands, *The Wind* is in fact rather playful with the question of whether we see Letty's projections and premonitions, or simply a vivid rendering of *where she is*.

This question is posed very early on, in the film's first scene. Letty is alone on a train; her pale beauty and incongruously prim manner attract the attention of a fellow passenger, cattle trader Wirt Roddy (Montagu Love). When Letty is taken aback by a gust of wind through the train window, Roddy steps in with ostentatious gallantry, brushes her down, and takes the opportunity to sit beside her. As a conversation develops, Letty glances out of the window at the enveloping dust storm, prompting the first shot in the film from Letty's point of view, and she says – as if in passing, to fill a potentially awkward silence – that she wishes the wind would stop. Roddy takes the opportunity to playfully intimidate her, invoking local 'injun' folklore and describing how women are liable to 'go crazy' amongst the never-ending winds. To Letty's left is a window onto a strange and threatening new land, and to her right is a cynical and intimidating older man, so she understandably grows anxious. And when Letty next looks out at the storm, and we see a second point-of-view shot, something has changed; graphically, the image is virtually identical to the first, but this character's view of the environment has now been fundamentally conjoined with threats and mysteries of a different order. Letty physically recoils. She now sees not only unwelcoming conditions, but intuits the prospect of social and sexual violence. Accordingly, audiences of *The Wind* are from the beginning made uncertain about how to 'place' its images and sequences of ferocious weather – as a context for, or as a projection of, Letty's ordeal. This strategy is capitalised on most fully in a climactic rape sequence, when an intense storm and a male attacker come together in both a metaphorical and a literal sense.

It would be quite misleading, though, to suggest that Victor Sjöström's film is somehow dominated by the experiential perspective of Letty, or that the world we see is *her* world. To use the terms offered by David Bordwell and Kristin Thompson, *The Wind* does not consistently provide us 'deep' access to Letty and her 'inner images' (2001: 73). One sequence in particular in fact denies us that access at a point in the narrative when Letty's subjective experience is of considerable interest and importance. Shortly after reluctantly marrying a cattle farmer, Lige (Lars Hanson), Letty is about to be left alone in an isolated shack (her new home), while Lige joins an expedition of cattlemen braving the intense wind (they are venturing out to find ways of preventing imminent famine). Deeply fearful of being home alone with the incessant wind, Letty asks Lige to let her join them. The two ride out to join the party, but before long it becomes clear that Letty is physically incapable of staying the course. She soon loses control of her horse, and has to ride on Lige's, clutching him for support and protection; later she falls to the ground, and is escorted back home by Lige's friend. These are crucial experiences for Letty. Afraid of the psychological threat posed by the wind, she attempts to 'take it on' physically, and fails.

But the film presents these moments as events rather than personal experiences. Put very simply, almost all of the exterior action described above is staged and filmed in long-shot or medium-shot set ups. When Letty falls from the horse, or when she seems to plead with Lige to let her remain with the riding party, these moments are not given the slightest subjective inflection. For much of the sequence, we can barely see her face. Indeed, many of the actors' gestures and movements are harder to identify and interpret because of the extreme dust storm. And for a handful of minutes, we seem to be watching footage of people struggling to carry out physical actions (mounting and dismounting horses, keeping hold of their headwear), a sensation which would no doubt be borne out by details of on-location struggles. This is not the place or the time for a carefully managed close up!

Fig. 6: A record of
people struggling:
The Wind (1928)

However much we sense a temporary suspension of narrative, prompted by extraordinarily vivid images of bodies in an extreme environment, it is important to remember that this effect still has narrative implications. We are, for a time, less closely aligned with Letty's experience of the wind, and more likely to see the weather as a kind of objective circumstance suffered by everyone in the story. The extent to which environmental experience is a shared experience is a vital question posed by *The Wind*.

Local Hero

The premise of *Local Hero* is built on a relatively schematic opposition between environmental values; that of a small, rural community versus a large, profit-driven (and foreign) oil corporation. But it weaves from this a surprisingly ironic and nuanced reflection on questions of nature, culture, locality and resource. Mac MacIntyre (Peter Riegert) is a young and ambitious employee at a large Texan oil firm, sent by the company's Chief Executive, Felix Happer (Burt Lancaster) to a small Scottish town, Ferness. Mac's mission is to buy up the town, freeing access to the off-shore oil. It is perhaps no surprise that Mac's venture does not go entirely to plan, undermined, in part, by his growing affection for Ferness and its community. But *Local Hero* does not just stage a victory for the proverbial small guy against greed, and in fact could be described as having a rather despondent political message. What makes the film's environmental narrative so interesting is rather its insistence that there is no 'real' or 'raw' nature untouched by human interest or mediation – instead there is a range of more or less harmful and absurd perspectives through which people understand their physical and atmospheric surroundings.

Unlike *The Wind*, which follows an unprepared individual as she confronts and is transformed by the brute elemental force of an unfamiliar environment, an environment which has a relatively coherent character and agency, *Local Hero* leaves open the question of determinacy. Yes, Ferness changes and affects Mac, but it is difficult to point to moments or details when this change takes place, or to confidently interpret the depth of these effects. Rather than stage moments of communion or conflict between person and place, *Local Hero* shows us the messy variety of ways, from farce to transcendence, in which someone might grow to understand their surroundings in non-anthropocentric terms. Everybody seems to have a stake in Ferness, and finds in this environment their own set of properties and connotations.

Local Hero has fun playing these worldviews off against one another, not least in a scene shortly after Mac arrives in Scotland. Before visiting Ferness itself, Mac stops off at the Aberdeen headquarters of Knox Oil and Gas, accompanied by Danny Oldsen (Peter Capaldi), a local Knox employee and Mac's appointed guide. Two enthusiastic engineers, working in a kind of aquatic laboratory, show Mac and Danny a scale model of Ferness, and demonstrate with comic ease how the built community will be replaced by a refinery – all it takes is removing one item, and slotting in another (an irony apparently lost on the engineers). But the demonstration is interrupted by a female laboratory assistant, Marina (Jenny Seagrove), who has come to fix a fault in the pool. She strips down to her swimwear, and dives athletically into the water, distracting the visitors (in particular Danny) from their business. This intervention is more than facile titillation, though; combined with the already absurdist quality of the scene, Marina's presence has more surreal than erotic currency. Bill Forsyth's direction does not invite us to dwell on the philosophical oddness or complexity of this moment (throughout, his style is very unobtrusive), in which onlookers are shifting their gaze between a plastic model and a living women sharing the same body of water. By the end of *Local Hero*, audiences are encouraged to suppose that Marina may well be a mermaid, but this is not something which *triumphs over* the instrumentalist worldview expounded by the engineers. It is just another way of being there.

Fig. 7: Ferness as a model: *Local Hero* (1983)

How is this variability manifest in the structure and content of the film's narrative? As was the case with Letty and the opening of *The Wind*, it is a significant storytelling decision not to grant audiences of *Local Hero* access to Ferness before Mac arrives. The opening credits of the film establish an urban-Texas setting in a very straightforward manner (big and busy roads, local-radio weather reports, etc), and one could well imagine an equivalent, mirroring sequence showing us 'everyday' Ferness. The decision to withhold the town's appearance until Mac actually arrives there is partly about aligning our perspective with that of the main protagonist, then. But we can be more specific than this; *Local Hero* forgoes the opportunity to establish rural Scotland as an environment which suffers intrusion, as a 'garden' into which an environmentally disruptive 'machine' enters (to borrow the terms of Leo Marx). Instead, the locality emerges to Mac and the viewer in a series of impressions.

This effect is made possible by the fact that Mac is something of a cipher or an empty vessel. Brief sequences of him at home or interacting with friends and colleagues give us not very much other than the vague impression of a financially successful young man who would like to be even more so. Although he is the film's central character, we credit Mac with little agency or creative ambition, little insight or imagination (and audiences are likely to have few strong associations with the actor's other roles). As a result, those moments in which Mac is fleetingly awakened to the richness of this new place – when, for example, he gets distracted from his deal-making by a pleasant sunset, or when he walks bare-foot along the beach – lead to very little.

Mac is not a man whose experiences are likely to be transformed or enlarged by details of place, and in this respect his character could be usefully contrasted with that of Joan Webster (Wendy Hiller) in Michael Powell and Emeric Pressburger's *I Know Where I'm Going!* (1945). Like Mac, Joan is established as a focused, materialistic and city-based person who heads to rural Scotland with a plan – a plan which inevitably unravels. (The films even illustrate this in similarly symbolic moments; Joan loses her printed itinerary to the ocean, while Mac leaves his watch in a rock pool.) Joan is all set to marry a rich older man, but the weather forces her to delay a boat trip to the island of Kiloran on which her fiancé waits, across the water from the Isle of Mull. Unlike the brutal and unforgiving wind suffered by Letty in *The Wind*, the weather here has a playful and conspiratorial agency, encouraging Joan's union with Torquil MacNeil (Roger Livesey). She is at times stubborn and proud, but always seems open (or potentially open) to the people and places, customs and legends, of Mull. Mac in *Local Hero* is more indifferent, and although his mission becomes confused and waylaid, his loosening grip on authority lacks a concomitant awakening. It is an interesting feature of the film that Mac's worldview, his relationship to the place he has come to, is not reinvigorated to the extent we might hope or expect.

But we should not mistake this for a paucity of environmental imagination on the part of *Local Hero*. Instead, the film places Mac in a fascinating binary relationship with Felix Happer. As the man in charge of a large Texan oil firm, a firm vigorously expanding into apparently pristine areas, Happer is a capitalist in whom we would expect to find little sympathy for non-human concerns. But he is, rather incongruously, a dedicated astronomer,

Fig. 8: Mac's watch
succumbs to
the ocean:
Local Hero (1983)

a man with little or no apparent concern for business, and a perfect dramatic foil to Mac's perfunctoriness. The film introduces Happer by way of a scene in which the company's board meet to discuss the Scottish drilling initiative. One man is explaining the proposals as he points to a map of the Scottish coast. Happer is present, but asleep. We of course cannot say whether he is dreaming of Scotland, but there is a definite sense that plans and maps are somehow ill-suited to Happer's philosophy, and that he understands and envisions his world in ways fundamentally different to those around him. When briefing Mac on his overseas trip, Happer instructs him to watch the sky (telling him to look up, when Mac surely *should*, from a strategic point of view, look down). And in a surreal parody of malevolent Bond villains, Happer's luxurious office is equipped with a private planetarium, unveiled at the flick of a switch; an extraordinarily peculiar combination of wealth, power and awestruck humility.

Perhaps the most interesting of these character quirks is the fact that Happer does not seem to operate on a day-to-day or present-tense time scale, and instead talks of the past and the future, as if tuned into cycles completely removed from ongoing social developments and transactions. Ralph Waldo Emerson once speculated about how enthralled people would be if the stars only appeared one night in every thousand years (2003: 37), and Happer gives us a little of that sense – as if he has not quite been socialised. We are used to seeing film characters ignore environmental despoliation through ignorance or greed, but it is unusual to see such a character adopt such a vast perspective, a worldview in which astronomical mysteries dwarf the relative trivialities of one planet's cleanliness. The fact that he has achieved the luxurious position from which to think like this by way of relentless and profit-driven natural-resource extraction only adds to the story's many ironies.

The film's resolution, in which Happer commits to building at Ferness a research facility concerned with space *and* oceanic exploration, is an attempt to square some of its circles. It is an interesting note on which to end *Local Hero*, but by no means normalises Happer's genuinely strange environmental ethics. He is not the film's main character, but the combination of oddness and power he exerts over Mac (and in turn the film) is vital. Mac, as I have claimed, is something of a blank slate, and his attempts to see in Ferness what Happer *wants* him to see are pathetic. Neither man is a reassuring guide to the world.

The Headless Woman

The Wind, as we saw, is a story of one lonely woman's exposure to an extreme and terrifying environment. *The Headless Woman* is almost the opposite; it is about a woman, Verónica (María Onetto), surrounded to the point of suffocation by family members, acquaintances, and the various conveniences of modern life. In *The Wind*, doors and windows are precarious, under siege from natural forces which threaten to overwhelm the characters at any given moment; people in *The Headless Woman* navigate comfortable and familiar homes, commenting on and observing the weather from locations of comfort and safety. Nature in this film is not an immediate threat, nor does it have a directly causal role in the narrative, but it becomes important in oblique and indirect ways. *The Headless Woman* challenges us to think about what kinds of agency and significance environmental details can take on in a film when they don't announce themselves in the form of spectacular weather or determining landscape.

The story is not a complex one. In the film's third sequence, Verónica is driving her car, gets distracted by the ringing of her mobile phone, and accidentally hits someone or something in the road. Too shocked or scared to leave her car and investigate, Verónica (like the film's audience) remains suspended in uncertainty about the consequences of her collision – did she strike an animal or a child? From this point on, *The Headless Woman* includes very little narrative activity. Verónica is dazed and uncommunicative, although the reactions of other people suggest that this isn't out of character for her. The attempts of her husband and his cousin to cover up the crime, if indeed one has been committed, only take the form of phone conversations, to which we have little visual or aural access. Michael Haneke's *Caché* (*Hidden*, 2005), a film with similar formal and thematic interests to *The Headless Woman*, develops a very suspenseful narrative from a comparable premise; a white, privileged family is unable and unwilling to confront their culpability in violent but dimly understood events. Haneke extracts the tension from this situation and explores its web of implications, but Martel instead uses the situation as a prompt to observe the routine actions and exchanges of a social milieu. Instead of a plot, the film develops a kind of pressurised quotidian.

This pressure is only partly caused by Verónica's road accident and its aftermath. There is also a string of details concerning the characters' material environment – more specifically, the technological management of that environment – whose relation to Verónica's predicament are obscure but undeniable. The film begins with young boys playing in and around a barren canal; shortly after Verónica's accident, a rainstorm hits the local town; women gossip about, and attend, a newly opened swimming pool that may have been contaminated by an adjacent vet surgery; heat and water supplies malfunction; a major sewage pipe is blocked by an unidentified dead body; a labouring gardener discovers remnants of a fountain or pool besides Verónica's house. These details tend not to progress the narrative as such, but almost all are experienced or learned about by Verónica, and their cumulative effect on her – and on her inability to 'move on' – is profound. Sophie Mayer even claims that the film's entire diegsis is 'framed, structured and delimited by the municipal pipes' (2014: 199).

One of the narrative's crucial sequences in this respect occurs roughly two-thirds through the film. At this point, Verónica has seemed to be gradually improving; her bemusement and dislocation from the world have started to ease, and she appears to be enjoying a brief trip with family members. Sitting in the back of a car, possibly asleep, the head of a young woman gently resting on her shoulder, Verónica has reached some sort of peace. But the formal organisation of the scene (including the sound of the radio, the light, the landscape rolling by) recollects that moment earlier on when Verónica suffered her collision, and sure enough she is once again rudely awakened from her distracted contentment. As the car drives alongside the canal, a small gathering of emergency-service vehicles and per-

Fig. 9: Verónica's garden: *The Headless Woman* (2008)

49

sonnel comes into view; the four women in the car look on, and the camera is gradually re-positioned to leave only Verónica in the frame, gazing out the car window at the search party and the canal, presumably wondering about her own possible involvement in the situation. They drive close by, and learn from another onlooker that the sewer has been blocked – probably by a dead body.

In the narrative design of *The Headless Woman*, this is an important sequence. Verónica and the audience learn that some sort of accidental killing has probably occurred in this area (which looks to our eyes almost identical to the site of Verónica's original collision; she herself will know more than us about the proximity). There are few diegetic facts that Martel establishes as clearly as this, and few scenes in the film in which Verónica becomes visibly aware of, or reacts to, new information or circumstances. In turn, we are able to see very clearly how Verónica and those close to her are willing and able to remain blind to and detached from difficulties beyond their comfort zone. The women decide to close the car windows as they drive by, to escape the stench. Because the camera remains, as it does for so much of the film, in the vicinity of Verónica, we do not see the sewer or what blocks it, just as we did not see who or what was struck down by her own car. Both scenes stage a dynamic relationship between violence and myopia, but the second time round this failure to witness is given a more tangible, environmental resonance. The stench and dirt of the event render it conveniently inaccessible and out of bounds for Verónica and her family.

It is not uncommon for narratives to locate acts of death and violence in unpleasant conditions – sites of ugliness, of refuse, of discomfort or of bland anonymity. I would suggest that *The Headless Woman* adds another degree of environmental complexity to this convention by locating its crime scene in a network of causes and effects. In studies of narrative, the term 'network' is usually applied to stories in which a variety of characters and locales intersect in complex and sometimes ingenuous ways. In Martel's film, there is a stronger sense of material connections, albeit stubbornly mysterious ones. Is this the same infrastructure which supports the apparently polluted swimming pool, or the drinking water of the girl suffering from hepatitis, or the fountain in Verónica's own garden? By keeping in play these possibilities, *The Headless Woman* ensures that Verónica's culpability is inescapable but unlocatable.

María Onetto's performance in the film as Verónica has been likened to the roles played by Monica Vitti in the films of Michelangelo Antonioni; both women are alienated, beautiful, almost ethereal witnesses of events and experiences. John Orr characterises the 'plight of Vitti' in ways which certainly chime with *The Headless Woman*: 'a crucial member of the nuclear family, openly prosperous, endures breakdown through the breakdown of technologies which help to make their families prosperous' (1998: 46). But the contrasts are revealing. Vitti's performances, especially as Vittoria in *L'Eclisse* (1962), show us a woman confronting a series of seemingly disconnected human actions and material spaces; sometimes these abstracted phenomena seem to delight Vitti's women, and sometimes they are terrifying. In *L'Eclisse*, the expensive sports car of Vittoria's male suitor is stolen by a drunk man and driven to a reservoir. When, the following morning, the car and corpse are dredged up, Vittoria seems disturbed by the accident and the behaviour of onlookers, but she is in attendance as a kind of existentially removed visitor, with no stake in the actions and repercussions of an event like this. Verónica only wishes she could be so disinterested. In *The Headless Woman*, the public discovery of a dead body is not a metaphysical event, but something physically entangled with the world and its workings.

3   FILM GENRE AND THE NATURAL ENVIRONMENT

Genres could be said to enable and encourage a patterned emphasis on certain formal and narrative features. Sometimes this emphasis falls on, or incorporates, non-human agency and contexts – as in disaster movies and westerns. In these films, there is a strong likelihood of characters having to deal with the fact that human control and design has important limits. However, bringing an environmental alertness to studies of film genre need not – and should not – be a case of focusing exclusively on those categories of film where apparently natural settings gain prominence, or when nature is oriented against human life in sharp binary terms. This chapter will consider how a number of familiar genres operate according to certain environmental parameters and expectations, even when nature does not seem to be thematically or narratively central; it will then explore in detail the example of film noir.

Tangible genres

A disaster film such as *Aftershock* (2012) unsurprisingly makes non-human agency a spectacular and dominating presence; a domestic melodrama, such as *This Happy Breed* (1944), unsurprisingly, does not. But what of a film such as *Force Majeure* (briefly discussed in Chapter 2), in which the framework of a domestic melodrama – marital discord, pathos, sexual politics – is momentarily injected with disaster-film iconography? Or indeed *The Big Lebowski* (1998), whose opening shot invokes the western genre, tracking across anonymous and seemingly timeless scrubland (accompanied by the song 'Tumbling Tumble Weeds'), before eventually arriving at a vista of late-twentieth-century Los Angeles? In moments such as these, genres seem almost to come into physical contact with one another. Watching them, we are reminded that film genres organise and deploy the environment in carefully circumscribed ways, and that imaginative filmmakers can choose to expand on or experiment with these patterns to achieve particular effects. In the same way that stars and costumes are often generic, and so are ripe for repetition, variation and subversion, so physical conditions are part of a genre's field of characteristics.

Anis Bawarshi describes genres themselves as 'rhetorical ecosystems' (2001: 70), and writes of the ways 'in which we perceive particular environments as requiring certain immediate and "appropriate" attention and responses' (2001: 77). After all, it is common to talk of genres as 'worlds' whose invisible rules dictate relations and activities, generating a kind of internal plausibility, or verisimilitude. Of course, a genre's verisimilitude is normally conceived of mainly in social and cultural terms – patterns of behaviour that become desired and expected – but such activities always take place somewhere. John Frow suggests that we could define genre as a 'relationship between textual structures and the situations that occasion them' (2006: 13), and although he is referring to real-world situations that bring about certain norms (meeting a neighbour for the first time, teaching your child to swim), I believe the term 'situation' could also be taken to mean something like a fictional setting – such as a courtroom or a desert – common to a number of generically related texts.

As Frow goes on to explain, 'far from being merely "stylistic" devices, genres create effects of reality and truth which are central to the different ways the world is understood' (2006: 19). According to this expanded understanding of genre, our experience of fictional narratives *and* real life are never quite as open as we might imagine; our cultural knowledge is bound by (generic) parameters of seeing and thinking. A genre's worldview is not only to be found in texts, and neither is it purely or exclusively about people.

For many of the reasons outlined in Chapter 1, the medium of film is especially likely to lend its genres a vividly and consistently located quality. A comic short story or a painted portrait might well be rigorously focused on people, and more or less immune to the world beyond the immediate vicinity of human minds and bodies. But a comic film or a biopic, meanwhile, is very unlikely to be so absolutely anthropocentric in its scope, and will almost certainly arrange its human activity within and against non-human contexts. This chapter will ask what role environmental conditions play in the identity of film genres. How do these notoriously amorphous groupings of texts collectively and creatively organise their worlds? In what ways can film genres be understood as negotiations with worldly, environmental subjects?

Daniel Yacavone provides one possible approach to this topic in *Film Worlds: A Philosophical Aesthetics of Cinema* (2014). Although Yacavone's study is not especially concerned with environmental subjects or approaches, it does raise interesting questions about the philosophical and aesthetic 'work' undertaken by a text or a group of texts in their efforts to make a world for us to view. More specifically, Yacavone borrows a scheme or rubric from the philosopher Nelson Goodman, whose *Ways of Worldmaking* (1978) identifies five processes for 'meaningful, intentional world creation' (2014: 87):

- composition/decomposition
- weighting (or emphasis)
- ordering
- supplementation/deletion
- deformation (or distortion)

Yacavone and Goodman are more concerned with the distinctions between imaginative worlds than what distinguishes an imaginative world from the real world. But the categories with which they work are very useful for thinking about what film genres make of, and with, *our* world. They can be roughly adapted into the following questions:

- How does a genre tend to visually and aurally frame its world?
- What qualities of the world does a genre emphasise?
- In what order do we see/experience/learn of different elements of a genre's world?
- What has this genre added to/subtracted from our world in order to

create its own?
- How does one genre or generic text engage with and reformulate another?

As Yacavone notes, these intersect and overlap substantially. Taken together, they provide a very useful starting point for thinking about how the relationship between the world and a genre is, in the words of Steve Neale, 'necessarily continuous', and how the influence of that world 'can be detected even where genres themselves are at their most self-consciously self-referential' (2003: 213). In short, a genre's artifice and contrivance does not prevent us from asking about its relationship to real-world features and referents.

Take, for example, the road movie. The question is not whether its vision of the natural environment is valid or profound, but rather how it becomes, and makes sense as, a genre in part *through* its environmental imagination. To return to the terms of Yacavone and Goodman, we can say that the road movie

- tends to frame landscapes through vehicles, and according to man-made boundaries and markers, such as roads and borders;
- emphasises distance and monotony;
- uses narrative structure to posit open spaces as a (longed for) refuge from social pressures;
- tends to eliminate or downplay rural labour and industry;
- often makes extensive use of popular music, resituating familiar words and music to incongruous or revealing effect.

Of course, when we turn to striking examples of the genre – *Smultronstället* (*Wild Strawberries*, 1957), *Pierrot le fou* (1965), *Two-Lane Blacktop* (1971), *Zhantai* (*Platform*, 2000) – it soon becomes clear that they do not slavishly adhere to such processes. But however disparate and independently distinctive these examples might be, they can still be said to envisage the natural world according to ideas and formulae which extend way beyond their own boundaries as texts. Or, to put this another way, we cannot help but view and interpret their worlds as somehow constructed by, and beholden to, generic forces. Given that much of the language used in film genre studies emphasises the medium's symbolic, semantic and syntactic effects, it is important to remember this other side of the equation – the ways in which such effects are invariably rooted in, contingent on, and even productive of, worldly qualities; 'genre,' writes Bawarshi, 'is both the boundary and the presencing, both the ideological construction of an environment and its rhetorical enactment' (2001: 78).

The western is an unavoidable point of reference here. Not only is it often thought to be the most clearly demarcated of all film genres, but it is also one with a vivid and ever-present – though unstable and inconsistent – environmental dynamic. (It is interesting to consider the extent to which these two are related.) As such, it has inevitably attracted ecocritical attention; in her introduction to the edited collection, *The Landscape of Hollywood Westerns*, Deborah A. Carmichael describes the genre as offering 'a unique opportunity to explore both current and historical perspectives on the role of nature in nation building and national identity' (2006: 15), and this opportunity has been taken up by a number of scholars, including Robin L. Murray and Joseph K. Heumann in their *Gunfight at the Eco-Corral* (2012). (Needless to say, this discussion can be taken to work far beyond Hollywood; see, for example, *Yojimbo* (1961) and *El Topo* (1970).) Horror has also been studied as a genre with considerable interest in images and ideas of nature, though this tends to manifest itself in a particular sub-genre, sometimes known as 'eco horror' – examples of which include *The Crazies* (1973), *Gwoemul* (*The Host*, 2006) and *Antichrist* (2008) – rather than as a consistent preoccupation or precondition.

Film noir

Film noir does not have the deep and direct connection to environmental politics and subjects that the western does, and it is far less likely than the horror film to explore in depth the uneasy distinction between human and non-human agency. But it is a genre so intent on delimiting a part of the world as its own, and on revealing the often pathetic lack of control that people have over that world, that its material environment tends to accrue a surprising significance. I have chosen to discuss it at length in this chapter not because it is the film genre most concerned with nature, but precisely because its environmental poetics are latent. We have the opportunity to discover, rather than simply chronicle, how and why the environment matters in film noir.

Many of the most treasured and most acclaimed examples of film noir seem not to invite or repay sustained attention to environmental qualities. And so a great many interpretive and analytical frameworks for dealing with the genre have found little or no need to dwell on questions or details of the non-human material world. There is so much to say about noir's social and aesthetic character – its knotted sexual politics (Kaplan 1998), its relationship to World War II (Biesen 2005), its racial project (Lott 1997), its philosophical preoccupations (Pippin 2012) – that surveys of the genre might very well not attend to its environmental character at all. We are not really obliged to watch these films and ask of them ecocritical questions. They instead seem to be about epistemology, psychosis, fate, eroticism, capitalism, irony; human energies and dilemmas. Film noir could be said to fit largely in the tradition described by Leo Braudy as that of the closed film (exemplified for Braudy by the work of Fritz Lang, who directed many great noirs), in which 'the world of the film is the only thing which exists' (2002: 46), and whose constituent parts are fabricated and manipulated, rather than welcomed in from the world at large.

But if there is a core line of noir interpretation, exploring its socio-logical, psychoanalytical and ideological character, there is also what we might call a 'second order' of concerns, clustered around noir's textural tangibility, and our sense of it as a strikingly grounded mode. Historically, American film noir had a stronger geographical and locational realism than many other Hollywood genres, exploring (in particular) Californian urban and suburban environments with a relish and a specificity unmatched in, for example, horror films and musicals. It has also been understood as a phenomenologically rich genre, which is to say that it is often invested in tactility and texture (office furniture, rain-soaked streets), and on charac-ters' embeddedness in a world of palpable objects and surfaces. Henrik Gustafsson connects these qualities to the genre's storytelling strategies, explaining that 'its heavy emphasis on subjective experience augmented by first-person point-of-view, voice-over, and flashbacks solicits a phenom-enological focus on the sensory engagement with space' (2013: 51–2). Noir stories are told and filmed in such a way that physical contexts are almost never neutral or inert. And because these contexts are often apparently *unnatural* in their key characteristics – electric lighting, mechanised trans-port, claustrophobic architectural spaces – the noir mode is one in which environmental features can take on considerable energy and significance.

The Movie Book of Film Noir features two chapters by Deborah Thomas; the first charts the genre's navigation of post-war male anxiety, but the second (which immediately follows the first) is presented as a chronicle of precisely those effects and pleasures which escape sociological definition, details which can only be found in the 'nooks and crannies of the films' imagery and language' (1992: 71). Describing and classifying these qualities, Thomas is drawn to physical, spatial and textural terms such as 'boundaries', 'solidity', 'blockage' and 'flow'. These tend to have a metaphorical currency in her analyses, but they also describe aspects of the film worlds themselves:

> Noir men are typically tired (or are lured by others wanting or advo
> cating peace and rest) and are easily drawn in to the tantalizing
> shapelessness of sleep, forgetfulness, and even death. It is in
> this connection that the imagery of water often pointed out as so
> prevalent in film noir is important: on the one hand, solidity and
> potential fragmentation, on the other hand, liquidity and merging,
> an end to the effort of holding oneself together lest one crack into
> pieces. (1992: 78)

Paul Schrader was one writer who had identified the importance of water in the genre, noting in his influential 'Notes on Film Noir' 'an almost Freudian attachment to water' (1996: 57), as well as a tendency in the films' lighting to give equal emphasis to human characters and their settings. Some of the examples explored later in this chapter will further develop the question of how and why water has accumulated a kind of privileged status in film noir.

As James Narmeore demonstrates in his exhaustive study of noir, *More Than Night: Film Noir in Its Contexts* (1998), the genre can only be properly understood in relation to non-filmic contexts and practice. Of these, so-called 'hard-boiled' fiction is the one most often cited, as an explicit and implicit source of a great many noir films. While it is not difficult to identify 'key ingredients' in the novels and stories of Dashiel Hammett, James M. Cain and Raymond Chandler (many of which have become clichés more cloying than those of other genres), Frederic Jameson's writing on Chandler helps us look beyond dialogue, action and character toward important spatial and material forces at work. For example, Jameson suggests that the geography of Los Angeles prompts Chandler to develop a coexistence between the 'urban' and the 'natural' 'in which neither is effaced by the other' (2016: 48). *The Big Sleep*, perhaps Chandler's most famous novel, offers

> a visual fever chart of weather: clouds, drizzle, bright sun, fog, heavy rain and automobile lights in the darkness; a sequence which has its own logic and about which it would be premature indeed to suppose that – following the old 'expressive fallacy' – it entertained any meaningful symbolic relationship with the sequence of human events taking place simultaneously in urban space proper. (2016: 49)

Jameson also writes in particular about the ocean in the closing passages of *Farewell, My Lovely*, which 'glitters with all that mineral fascination, that radically non-human, cold, even unnatural mystery that the ocean often has in writers who do not specialize in sea-stories, or in cultures which are non-maritime' (2016: 84). *The Big Sleep*, meanwhile, climaxes at an inland location, but Jameson suggests that the presence of pouring rain 'restores the watery element that is the sign of the non-human axis of matter in these novels' (2016: 86).

These interpretations cannot, of course, be straightforwardly transplanted onto the genre's films. They are, though, in rather striking accordance with Schrader, Thomas, Gustafsson and others, all of whom diagnose the nature of noir not so much in the rhetoric or even in the structuring of its films, but rather in momentary details and intrusions. In the films discussed below, we will find examples of such moments – but also cases in which the natural environment exerts a considerable and sustained influence over the films' shape and character.

I have chosen to draw on examples from different periods and different global contexts. This is not to deny the fact that mid-century Hollywood crime films hold a privileged position in the semantic field of noir, but rather to respond to the fact that the genre's spirit and logic has been adapted to a variety of environments. Fascinating on their own terms, these films also help us build a more substantial account of noir's tendencies and affordances, and a fuller picture of how it responds to and orders the world. Although I have done this in a broadly chronological manner, I make no claims for this representing a development or a trajectory. I approach the films with ecocritical questions which I believe are helpful for thinking about their environmentality, but which are not offered as interpretive keys for entire periods or waves of noir production.

Delusion and absolution in classical noir

High Sierra (1941) was an important development in the emergence of Humphrey Bogart as a major figure in American cinema, and a vivid instance of early (or proto) film noir. Bogart plays professional robber Roy Earle, and the film begins with his release from prison. The first we see of him is the very moment he exits through the prison gate; Roy looks skywards and smiles, but his ease and satisfaction is sharply interrupted by the appearance of a man, whom we quickly take to be a criminal associate, sent to collect him upon his release. Roy opts to walk to the park instead of join this man in the car, because he wants to make sure that 'grass is still green and trees are still growing'. It is difficult to be certain whether this is Roy's genuine desire, or just a pointed refusal to follow orders (he will spend much of the film asserting what independence and moral authority he can). Either way, the subsequent sequence shows Roy enjoying a moment of genuine pleasure as he sits on a bench at the park. The audience, though, are shown a discarded newspaper on the grass behind Roy, the headline of which establishes his criminal past and identity. Taken together, these two short scenes provide a rather neat microcosm of the film's larger narrative design, one in which Roy's moral absolution will be accompanied by and enacted through a physical movement to open spaces – his final, climactic escape is to the film's eponymous mountain top.

This description suggests a rather crude and simple pastoralism, and *High Sierra* can be enjoyed and understood as a narrative which follows that familiar formula. Other influential noirs such as *The Asphalt Jungle* (1950) and *On Dangerous Ground* (1951) seem to follow a roughly similar blueprint, of the troubled urban male who needs fresh air and redemption, or fresh air *as* redemption. Jonathan F. Bell writes of noir heroes in such films as bringing 'their picnic baskets of angst out onto the open roads of rural America' (2000: 218). It is perhaps no surprise that a genre which habitually characterises urban space as threatening and unsettling would, almost by default, imagine non-urban environments as promising a kind of emancipation. That is what the men in these films hope to be granted. But Robert Pippin's *Fatalism in American Film Noir* (2012) has taught us not to take a noir hero's worldview at face value, or as evidence of the film's own philosophical and epistemological standpoint, and in this sense the ironies at play in the opening of *High Sierra* are telling. Roy's oblivious- ness to the newspaper lying nearby in the park is a case in point; it is as if the film is pointedly qualifying his play at innocence, which in any case was rather superficial (admiring the trees, throwing a ball to a group of children). And what were his reasons for coming to the park in the first place? Roy's claim that he wants see the grass and trees is inane, but more interestingly it is narcissistic, a self-aggrandising way of thinking about the world he is rejoining. It is not unlike honeymooners Eddie Taylor (Henry Fonda) and Joan Graham (Sylvia Sidney) in a famous scene in *You Only Live Once* (1937?), fooling themselves and each other (and us?) into believing that frogs are misunderstood romantics. In both films, we as viewers are tempted to indulge these characters and their longing for a kind of state- of-nature innocence, but it is typical of film noir (at its best) to retain a critical distance, and hint at the ineptitude of their fantasies.

Key Largo (1948) is less ambivalent than *High Sierra*; it features a Bogart character, Frank McCloud, whose goodness is more straightforward than Roy's, and whose relationship to the natural environment is more one dimensional. Frank is visiting the Hotel Largo in the Florida Keys to meet the father and widow of George Temple, with whom he served in the war. The hotel is also occupied by a criminal gang, headed by Johnny Rocco (Edward G. Robinson), masquerading as a fishing party. The mutual suspicion and inevitable clash between the two groups has a kind of environmental cor- relative in the form of a hurricane which strikes the island, compromising the escape by boat of Johnny and his criminal entourage. As far as film noir plots go, *Key Largo*'s is unusually contingent on environmental events, but in a rather schematic way: the storm is weathered and the innocent pre- vail; Frank outwits Johnny on a boat and navigates his way back to dry land, where his new love awaits. As Jameson and many others have noted, the noir world sometimes features coastal settings to generate a fascinating dissonance, a clash of scales, as seedy and labyrinthine stories play out – or more commonly culminate – alongside a monumental, independent and timeless ocean. *Mildred Pierce* (1945), *Kiss Me Deadly* (1955) and *The Long Goodbye* (1973) all achieve this to a greater or lesser extent. But Frank in *Key Largo* accomplishes a kind of mastery, or at least a victory, over his environment in a manner that does not draw on the genre's capacity for irony. He knows the world too well and is too sure of his position within it. It begs the question of whether a small-island setting is perhaps ill-suited to film noir; after all, islands are *already* places of isolation and vulnerability, and their narrative implications are fairly stable. They do not throw into relief a person's paranoia or self-delusion in the way that film noir so often does. They are too deterministic.

Niagara (1953) could similarly be accused of locating its narrative in an environment which is simply too straightforwardly significant. In many noir films, we are surprised by the sudden vividness and meaningful capacity of an unspectacular setting – the sewers of *He Walked by Night* (1948), the marshes in *Gun Crazy* (1950) – but not so with *Niagara* and its billboard location. Throughout, the film relies on the waterfall as a backdrop, a narrative setting, and as a famous profilmic point of reference (including all the cultural associations that come with it). The environmental context in *Niagara* is not latent, but overwhelmingly significant in a manner that is atypical of film noir. Familiar generic motifs and icons which we tend to associate with claustrophobic and anonymous spaces play out in a film world designed to evoke Romantic sublimity; the marriage is awkward, but the experiment is a fascinating one.

Joseph Cotten plays George Loomis, a veteran of the Korean War whose marriage to the adulterous Rose (Marilyn Monroe) has left him paranoid and despondent. The film begins, as a number of noirs do, with its hero at a point of despair and desperation. At first only a rocky landscape, crashing waterfall and a misty rainbow seem to be visible, but there is a small figure in grey moving towards the water. Subsequent shots and the introduction of a voice-over reveal this to be George. The voice-over is of course another noir convention, but here it seems to operate as a present-tense internal commentary rather than the more familiar retrospective address. Moreover, Cotten's calm, almost soothing tone works in deliberate disjunction with the on-screen action; as George approaches the foot of the falls and submits himself to a sensorial assault of noise and water and reflected light, he reflects on why he might be there in the first place:

Why should the falls drag me down here at 5 o'clock in the morning? To show me how big they are and how small I am? To remind me they can get along without any help? Alright, so they've proved it. But why not? They've had ten thousand years to get independent. What's so wonderful about that? I suppose I could too but it might take a little more time...

These final words are spoken as George has turned around and begun to walk away from the falls, providing some reassurance to viewers who assumed this was going to be a moment of ultimate despair, of suicide. Subsequent scenes give us more information with which to explain and contextualise George's actions, namely that his early-morning visit to the falls is not only a journey *towards* something, but also *away from* his secretive and maddening wife. The film treats George as a victim of both Rose and Niagara, as a simple sheep farmer who finds himself masochistically drawn to a beautiful, abusive woman and to a natural wonder which somehow compounds his anguish. This is an important point; George is painfully conscious of the fact that his fate is in some sense entwined with Niagara, but is its promise one of doom or of absolution? Does it mirror his anguish, stir his murderousness or anticipate his fall? As the plot of *Niagara* develops, these end up being almost indistinguishable – but that does not mean they are interchangeable. What threatens to be a crude symbol becomes something more interesting precisely because George himself struggles to interpret it.

As discussed in Chapter 2, a famous scene in *King Lear* has the king at the mercy of a wild storm whose meaning matters to the character as

Fig. 10: Between doom and absolution: *Niagara* (1953)

well as the audience. There is a broadly equivalent scene in *Niagara*, but it is not when George physically surrenders himself to the falls at the film's climax. Rather, it is when he meets Polly Cutler (Jean Peters), one of the honeymooners whose stay at Niagara overlaps with the Loomis's. Polly is a smart, modest and caring young woman who comes to George's cabin to treat his injured hand following his violently angry outburst, which had been deliberately provoked by Rose. The two have a frank exchange but clearly respect one another, and after a few minutes George turns off the light so Polly can properly see the multi-coloured illumination of the falls, of which the cabin offers an ideal view (albeit through noirish blinds). The scene teases us with the prospect of sexual tension and romantic promise, but these are held in check partly by George's absolute seriousness (Polly for the most part seems to respond to, rather than set, the tone). His offer to turn off the light is genuinely innocent, and there is nothing to suggest that he even understands this to be Polly's honeymoon. The spectacular back-drop does not prompt tenderness or passion, but rather a sober warning:

> Let me tell you something. You're young, you're in love. Well don't let it get out of hand like those falls over there. Up above ... did you ever see the river up above the falls? It's calm, easy. You throw in a log and it just floats around. Let it move a little further down and it gets going fast, and it hits some rocks, and in a minute it's in the lower rapids and nothing in the world – including God himself, I suppose – can keep it from going over the edge. It just *goes*.

For the natural environment to be so deliberately and self-consciously framed, as a visual and a narrative subject, is rare in film noir. The design and execution of this scene in *Niagara* in fact has more in common with the famous Universal melodramas of Douglas Sirk than with contemporary noirs such as *The Big Heat* (1953) or *The Big Combo* (1955); not unlike the wildlife motifs in Sirk's *All That Heaven Allows*, the falls in *Niagara* are an apparently simplistic metaphor whose meaning is never quite settled. In the scene between Polly and George, the falls take up their position in a mise-en-scène which seems to determine one set of meanings, only for George to respond to this with his own take on the environment.

Perhaps the most interesting aspect of how *Niagara* 'positions' the falls is the way in which the main character does not know how to engage

Fig. 11: An apparently simplistic metaphor: *Niagara* (1953)

with it. At first a solitary and reflective George is drawn to the waterfall, and seems to be on the verge of sacrificing himself; later, with Polly, he observes the falls as if from a cossetted box in an auditorium, attempting to extract a serviceable meaning from what he sees; finally, George is thrust over the precipice in his boat, after accidentally getting swept up in the river's current above the falls. The finale is a particularly deft coming together of environmental conditions and generic logic; George has already stated with utter clarity what happens to figures floating on the river as it approaches the falls (although at the time he was doing so metaphorically), and now he finds himself in that very position. And yet Cotten's performance in this final third is *not* that of a man consciously and willingly heading for disaster, but one who is helplessly being directed by sheer force of circumstance (the drift, the police pursuit, the running out of fuel) to his death – a quintessential noir trajectory. *Niagara* can by no means be understood as typical or representative of classical noir, but it does take to an extreme something which lurks more quietly in other films of the time, namely the tendency for troubled men to hope, in vain, for some kind of reconciliation between their situation and their environment.

Over exposure in art-film noir

In *Screening Modernism,* his comprehensive study of the rise of art cinema in post-war Europe, András Bálint Kovács identifies film noir as an important 'transitional step' between the classical and the modern, and argues that it makes perfect sense for this genre to have been a launching-off point for the careers of, amongst others, Luchino Visconti, Michelangelo Antonioni, Jean-Luc Godard and François Truffaut: 'The modernist idea that the narrative should serve merely as a frame that is filled in with expressive, emotional or intellectual material, the intensity of which is more important than the rational consistency of the narrative, proved to be a viable solution in film noir' (2007: 247). Kovacs relates this development to a broader shift in cinematic storytelling, namely the folding together of human acts and mental processes – the rise of subjective narration. No longer could audiences assume that the space-time they encountered in a film was some kind of absolute, disinterested or neutral context or container for actions and activities. *Hiroshima mon amour* (1959), *Persona* (1966) and *Sedmikrásky* (*Daisies*, 1966), for example, are not made up of consecutive verifiable events in the way that so many classical films are, but rather they are *renditions* which seem traceable to states of mind.

This mode of film narration, in which a character's consciousness holds significant sway over the presentation of action, tended to 'weaken the referential relationship between the world represented in the story and the empirical world' (2007: 244). The aesthetic possibilities of this, according to Kovacs, could be 'safely' explored in noir, a genre which allowed for some looseness of logic and rationality while still offering audiences (and filmmakers) a relatively stable and identifiable framework. I find this a convincing account of how and why the latent or qualified modernism of classical film noir would be taken up and built upon by ambitious European filmmakers, but it is one which regards narrative primarily as a system of information distribution and perspective. What, we might ask, became of the 'stuff' of noir – the objects and textures and environments – in this transition to a European art-film context?

Ossessione (*Obsession*, 1943) is a crucial work in this linage, not least because it rather neatly stages the meeting of American influence (James M. Cain's crime novel *The Postman Always Rings Twice* (1934)) and European authorship. It is also identified as a vivid marker of film-historical change by Gilles Deleuze, who early on in *Cinema 2: The Time-Image* writes of this film as marking a shift in what constituted a film 'situation'; in *Obsession* and subsequent Visconti films, writes Deleuze, 'objects and settings take on an autonomous, material reality which gives them an importance in themselves' (2005: 4). Gino (Massimo Girotti) is a poor and nomadic young man who, at an inn, meets and falls in love with its married proprietress, Giovanna (Clara Calamai). Unsure whether to choose the passion of Gino or the stability of her husband, Bregana (Dhia Cristiani), Giovanna eventually conspires with one (Gino) to kill the other (Bregana). The couple, though, cannot find happiness, and Giovanna is eventually killed in a car crash as the two of them flee from police.

If, as Kovacs suggests, noir lent itself to a move away from linear narratives propelled by human actions, then Visconti's debut film is a vital case in point. Its story has many film-noir features – adultery, masochism, fatalism, paranoia, irony – but the world of *Obsession* is not reduced to these as it seems to be in, for example, *Detour* (1945), an American noir with which it shares a number of qualities. Instead, the key locations in *Obsession* of the river and the road (between which sits the inn), and the documentary treatment they receive from Visconti, always nudge our awareness away from the melodramatic exchanges of the characters. 'It is as if the action floats in the situation,' writes Deleuze (2005: 4). According to Giuliana Minghelli, the road of *Obsession* is 'one of the first truly open spaces in the Italian cinema' (2008: 181).

Openness is a quality which seems to conjure up positive associations; open spaces, open minds, open hearts and open doors are for the most part more promising and more emboldening than their closed equivalents. But the distinction between openness and exposure is a fine one, and the people of film noir are so laden with guilt and secrecy that the prospect of space and visibility is not always a liberating one for them – and in many cases can prove to be quite the opposite. One of the most striking scenes in *Obsession* comes very near its climax; after trying to end their relationship, Gino has returned to the inn to confront Giovanna, believing her to have reported him to the police. Giovanna tells him the truth (she hasn't betrayed him, and is pregnant with his child), prompting Gino to leave. We next see the lovers at what appears to be the following morning, on the bleak, beach-like plain of the river. After a night of searching for him, Giovanna has found Gino wandering barefoot and aimless – a kind of abstracted reiteration of their first meeting. Gino talks in almost religious terms of his night spent walking this terrain and of having become a new man; the couple decide to leave together, and the vast unpeopled landscape might seem to chime with their vision of beginning again. But as well as vast, the environment has a flatness and a monotony which counterpoints their optimism. The river behind them is, after all, the same one into which Giovanni's husband fell to his death, and there is nothing in the gestures and the demeanour of the couple to suggest momentum or progress through and beyond this place, nor anything like a point-of-view construction showing Gino or Giovanni to be looking at their surroundings and discovering where they might lead. (From what we see, it is hard to even register the movement of the river.) The two of them have forgotten, or not quite realised, that the police continue to hunt Gino, and their naiveté is more pronounced than it would be in another setting precisely because this place makes us so aware of the couple's inertia and their exposure. They have mistaken space for promise.

Visconti's film pre-dates what is normally understood as the era of the European art film, and the positioning of noir characters in an exposed and an exposing landscape can be traced through to later films by, for example, Michelangelo Antonioni, Bertrand Tavernier and René Clément, as well as Hollywood films with a pronounced European influence, such as those by Robert Altman, Arthur Penn and Francis Ford Coppola. Antonioni's *Blow-Up* (1966), for example, may not often look like a film noir, and the brazen self-confidence of its central male, Thomas (David Hemmings), is an almost total inversion of the despair and pessimism we tend to see in film noir's broken men. But the structure of the film – in which a man encounters a beautiful woman embroiled in mysterious circumstances,

Fig. 12: Lovers with too much space: *Obsession* (1943)

and cannot fathom those circumstances – positions it somewhere on the branches of what Raymond Durgnat described in 1970 as 'the family tree of film noir'. And so the fact that its most vital location is a well-kempt urban park warrants attention as a conscious play with the genre's environmental conventions. It is here that Thomas first sees Jane (Vanessa Redgrave), photographs her secretive meeting with a man, and eventually finds a corpse.

Andrew Spicer, writing about European film noir, describes a 'dystopian sensibility that is fundamentally existential, evoking a malign and contingent universe' (2007: 15), but we find something more muted at the park in *Blow-Up*. It is a profoundly quiet place, an orderly (but not formal) design, distinguished by vivid and slightly monotonous greens, its trees and shrubbery gently animated by a soft breeze. However, while the film deliberately makes these affective details available to us, there is very little sense of what any of this has to do with Thomas, Jane and the situation in which they find themselves. The generally immobile camera and occasionally oblique framings do not allow a meaningful dynamic between people and place, figure and ground, to develop. The human narrative is neither determined by nor determinative of an environment, but simply *there,* in a place which Murray Pomerance aptly describes as one of 'eventlessness, poise, fixity' (2008: 224). What Thomas treats as an incidental backdrop to his photographic subject will become a stage on which his own doubts and confusions are exposed.

A number of European art films could be said to produce broadly similar effects, relocating film noir dynamics into colourful and airy environments, and in doing so introducing new uncertainties about the threats and tensions experienced by the characters. As one critic asked of Nuri Bilge Ceylan's *Bir Zamanlar Anadolu'da* (*Once Upon a Time in Anatolia*, 2011), 'why is this film noir so preoccupied with light?' (Wood 2012a: 18). The intense sun which is seen and felt throughout Bertrand Tavernier's *Coup de Torchon* (1981) only makes the sudden murderousness of its buffoonish main character (Philippe Noiret as Lucien Cordier) all the more absurdist and unsettling, while the similarly unrelenting brightness of *Plein Soleil* (1960) leaves us just as unsure about how to understand Tom Ripley (Alain Delon) and his own motivations for killing Phillipe Greenleaf (Maurice Ronet). In one of that film's key moments, Tom is left stranded on a small dinghy during a yachting trip, the result of a cruel and misjudged prank by Phillipe, whom Tom will soon murder. One could read it as a narrative sequence which motivates Tom's subsequent violence, an action which helps us understand more clearly his hatred of Phillipe. But seen in the broader context of art-film noir and its environmental aesthetics, the sun-drenched humiliation of Tom has rather different implications; alone on a small boat and in the brightest light one might imagine, this young man is no more knowable than he would be in more conventionally noirish settings. It is as if the film is pushing back against the genre's visual and spatial conventions as hard as it can, experimenting with a kind of environmental revisionism, but offering up nothing more hopeful or more lucid.

Neo-noir and material economies

When genres are adopted and developed in different parts of the world, the results can be, and often are, read as variations on and conversations with an 'original' Hollywood blueprint; that is how I have characterised European art-film noir. David Desser suggests that of all internationalised film genres, global noir is particularly animated by an 'impulse towards cinephilia', taking the form of a 'circuit of acknowledgements', allusions to an American-centric canon (2003: 528). But an environmentally-oriented approach to film study must of course acknowledge that films are not only texts amongst other texts, and that they are responses to and engagements with a material world. So *Coup de Torchon* is not only a creative upending of generic conventions; it is a film of and about West African climate and topography. And *Chinatown* (1974) is not only a Hollywood film continuing a certain Hollywood tradition (film noir); it is also a record of, and response to, certain localised conditions and politicised environments – namely the watersheds of Southern California. This is another way we can choose to approach the environmentality of film noir, by noting its capacity for 'plugging in' to the material economies of particular cities, regions and landscapes. Although it is true that a great many so-called 'neo-noirs' – such as *Blade Runner* (1982), *Strange Days* (1995) and *Dark City* (1998) – have embraced the genre's more baroque and expressionistic qualities, other noir films of recent decades have established and explored paranoia and intrigue as manifestations of real-world material conditions.

For example, a number of Chinese films which emerged around and since the turn of the twenty-first century have explored that country's notorious 'black economy' through a film noir framework. Films such as *Bari Yanhuo* (*Black Coal, Thin Ice*, 2014) and *Mangjing* (*Blind Shaft*, 2003) find in the genre an appropriate means of exploring the terrifying scale and anonymity of coal mining. They do not adopt an ethical position on the rights and wrongs of natural-resource extraction, but they do continue an important impulse of the classical noir tradition by seeking out those locations and environments in which rapid modernisation takes its toll – on people and places alike. In 'Lounge Time', her influential study of American noir and its rootedness in a post-war historical moment, Vivian Sobchack draws attention to the pertinence of certain non-domestic spaces (such as motels and diners) in noir, which she describes as 'chronotopes' distinguished by 'hyperbolized presence and overdetermined meaning' (1998: 130); the slag heaps and shipping containers of *Black Coal* and *Blind Shaft* have a similar agency and aptness which extend beyond their narrative function.

In the intricate and baroque *Black Coal*, these only occupy relatively little screen time; instead there is an expressionistic abundance of snow and ice, as well as certain familiar generic locales, such as a seedy night club decked out with mirrors. But it is the coal-mining context which prevents the film descending into a mannerist or overly derivative 'circuit of acknowledgements', and through which it retains the 'element of realism' that Carl Richardson, in his book *Autopsy* (1992), argues is the genre's life-support system. *Blind Shaft* is more straightforwardly realist, employing as it does certain conventions (such as the candid filming of non-professional performers, eye-level camerawork and the absence of music) which we associate with documentary, and with the urge to achieve a directness of experience and information which is normally compromised by generic conventions. In fact, *Blind Shaft* operates as a film which is as much naturalistic as it is realistic, drawing our attention to material details of miners' lives (where they sleep, how they wash) not for their intrinsic interest, but rather as evidence of an environmentally determined fate. J. Hoberman described the film as having the B-movie qualities of 'flavorsome reportage and the grit of daily life' (2004), and we should not misread this 'grit' as an immaterial aesthetic sensibility – it is an all-too-real constituent of daily experiences and environments. The rapid ascendency of Chinese capitalism has been possible because of the harvesting of fossil fuels on an almost unimaginable scale, and Chinese filmmakers have found in film noir a mode and worldview which is able to make this palpable at the level of humanist narratives.

The politics of *Blind Shaft* are its driving impulse, and contemporary China's material economy matters in the film to the extent that it governs the lives and livelihoods of marginalised and exploited people; this seems to be the project of the filmmaker Li Yang. In *Night Moves* (2013), an American film about the planning, execution and aftermath of an attack on a dam in Oregon, environmentalism and politics are much more boldly intertwined. Its noir characteristics, like those of *Blind Shaft,* are to be found in tone and outlook rather than mise-en-scène (as well as its title, which is inherited from Arthur Penn's desolate noir of 1975). A heist film whose protagonists are 'eco-saboteurs' rather than robbers or gangsters, *Night Moves* is not coy about the political pertinence of its subject matter. Early on, two of the three protagonists attend a screening of an amateur agitprop documentary about impending ecological catastrophe, and while filmmaker Kelly Reichardt is careful to clarify that neither of them seem particularly affected by it (Jesse Eisenberg's Josh is particularly unimpressed), the sequence nevertheless indicates a rather forthright approach on the part of *Night Moves* to confirm itself as part of a live, contemporary environmental discourse. A similar affect is achieved when one of the gang talks at length about marine biodiversity, or when another complains bitterly about the spread of golf courses and its catastrophic implications for the region's water. These are not digressions from the film's status and functioning as a wonderfully tense thriller, and neither are they solicitations by the film for us, as viewers, to become environmentally 'activated'. Instead, they are reminders that the paranoia and existential angst which are so important to noir's character can be rooted in a place and a time – a material economy and a living ecosystem.

4　NATIONAL CINEMAS AND THE NATURAL ENVIRONMENT

Chapter 3 asked how the natural environment could be said to affect and inform film genre, one of the most common means by which narrative cinema is categorised and interpreted. This final chapter asks similar questions of another crucial concept in film studies, and wider film culture: national cinema. For reasons I will explain in more detail, Japanese cinema offers itself as a particularly revealing case study for such a discussion, and we shall move towards an ecocritical interpretation of three Japanese films.

There is not the opportunity here to explore the vital debates about the relative efficacy of national cinema as an idea, and the simplifications and generalisations it can invite – but it would also be a mistake to pretend they didn't exist. After all, globalisation and postmodernity have exacerbated doubts about the already unstable notion of national identity, and questions of nationhood are perhaps even more vexed in the case of cinema than many other cultural forms, given the fact that movie production and distribution are global processes of baffling complexity. The volume and variety of work produced by national cinemas, and their uneven circulation around the world, can make it difficult to select and pursue a particular aspect in particular films with any confidence that they are indicative of larger currents.

In turn, this raises questions – similar to those common in genre studies – about the importance of representativeness; *O Thiassos (The*

Travelling Players, 1975) is not *like* many Greek films, and *London* (1994) is not *like* many British films, but does this compromise their usefulness or validity as examples of national cinema? There is rarely a neat way of rec-onciling richness with typicality, and the three Japanese films discussed at length towards the end of this chapter have been chosen for their intrinsic interest rather than their ability to reliably *stand for* other films – but they can nevertheless still be said to have clear and meaningful links to their national context. As I hope to demonstrate, these links can be understood more fully by attending to the films' engagement with the natural environ-ment.

However, if national cinema is always a subject plagued by meth-odological compromises, another difficulty comes to the fore when it is approached by way of environmental features and qualities – the risk of determinism. To claim that a certain nation's environmental condi-tions have a manifest effect on its cinema is to come dangerously close to a deeply problematic logic of purity, and seems to promote a vision of nationhood which is blind to the heterogeneity of collective identities. In a cautious pretext to his writing on determinism in environmental literature, Lawrence Buell warns that 'the theory of people and cultures as ecocontex-tual products may seem, and sometimes be, a pretext for ethnocentricity, imperialism, and racism' (2001: 130). Watchful of these risks, it is never-theless important to recognise that filmmakers working in different parts of the world not only function in contrasting cultural contexts, but may well also find themselves in vitally different natural environments – and that this too can inform their films.

Ecocontextual national cinemas

In his popular book about international politics, *Prisoners of Geography,* Tim Marshall claims that environmental conditions are the crucial – but often ignored – parameters dictating trade, diplomacy and warfare: 'geog-raphy has always been a prison of sorts, one that defines what a nation is or can be' (2015: 279). Climate, topography, natural barriers and points of access, navigable waterways, fossil fuels – these, according to Marshall, establish a non-negotiable context within which national leaders and their ideological ambitions must function. But as well as affecting a nation's political fate and culture, these same factors of course influence its creative expressions too. Russian geography did not determine the content of Anton Chekhov's writing, for example, but the tone and pathos of much of his work is not unrelated to the country's vast stretches of near-uninhabitable landscape. We tend to think of artists as responding to social shifts and emerging opportunities, but many are also likely to be engaging with the more-or-less constant facets of a given physical environment.

One way to begin thinking about the environmental character of a national cinema is to take stock of what those facets might be. Senegal is a country of sandy plains, and its capital city is mainland Africa's westernmost point. Bangladesh has approximately seven hundred rivers. The far north and south of Mexico are, geographically speaking, extremely different from one another. In and of themselves, these simple facts do not explain anything about the cinema of those nations, but they are an initial step towards a more nuanced understanding of those cinemas, and the sort of information which is very easily overlooked. Many important works in the canon of a national cinema may bear no obvious trace of these environmental characteristics, but just as many would be hard to imagine transposed or relocated to a physically different country.

That said, a film will almost certainly attend to only a tiny proportion of a nation's geography, and our awareness of large-scale characteristics will ideally be balanced by a sensitivity to more localised phenomena. These could be specific formations and locations, such as the swamps of Louisiana in the American South, or even certain environmental issues, such as the damming of the Yangtze River in China. Lúcia Nagib, whose writing on realism and global cinema we encountered in Chapter 1, argues that *Deus e o Diabo na Terra do Sol* (*Black God, White Devil*, 1964) is a film whose value and profundity as a Brazilian text is achieved, at least in part, through its knowing use of a very particular landscape, the *sertão* shrubland in the country's northeast. Nagib notes that the word 'Brazil' is not heard during the film, but far from interpreting this as an ambivalence about or turning away from nationhood as a concern, she instead focuses on how the *sertão* offers the director Glauber Rocha a literal and rhetorical grounding for the formal and ideological experiments he undertakes. More specifically, the extremely taxing physical experience, for cast and crew, of filming in these places contributes towards a 'revelatory realism' on which the film's 'national-identity effect' relies (2011: 52). Its closing sequence, in which the film's main character/actor runs across the *sertão* landscape,

Fig. 13: Brazil's sertão landscape: *Black God, White Devil* (1964)

is testament to a 'painful bodily experience and recognition of a harsh, cruel soil, under an unrelenting sun, which happens to be unmistakably located in Brazil' (2011: 64).

Nagib, it should be noted, finely balances an appreciation of the *sertão* as a physical place with a knowledge of its complex social, ideological and political associations in Brazilian society. Our appreciation and understanding of any national cinema will, likewise, be enriched by an awareness not just of a country's geography, but of its culturally inflected landscapes. In *Landscape and Memory,* his exhaustive chronicling of Western civilisation's environmental narratives and representations, Simon Schama argues that, rather than repudiate the cultural processes through which nature is mediated, 'it seems right to acknowledge that it is our shaping perception that makes the difference between raw matter and landscape' (1995: 10). On a very basic level, this could, for example, mean acknowledging the subtle distinctions between what is meant by the 'bush' and the 'outback' in Australia, or paying heed to the role of the forest in the German imagination. It would be difficult to adequately account for Fritz Lang's *Die Nibelungen: Siegfried* (*The Nibelungs*, 1924) without reflecting on what Schama calls the 'undeniable connections' in Germany 'between the mythic memory of the forest and militant nationalism' (1995: 119). It would also be interesting to ask whether such connections should have any bearing on our interpretation of German filmmaker Werner Herzog's use of woods, forests and jungles in countries far away from Germany. However, there are real risks here of crudely imposing simplistic predetermined meanings, and Herzog's films should serve as an important reminder that natural environments can inform a film's irony as well as its majesty or its realism.

Finally, an environmental approach to a national cinema might have reason to look outside the films themselves, and consider industrial trends and practices. For example, when and to what extent has location filming been a common practice? Has there been support and opportunities for a regionally various output? Which genres and modes are particularly important to a national cinema, and how have these emphasised (or overlooked) certain environmental characteristics? The prevalence of spectacular bodily movement and non-synchronous music in popular Hindi ('Bollywood') cinema generate conditions in which the natural environment is unlikely to be granted sustained prominence; the industrial conditions are different in France, where durational and locational realism have been more important to the design and production of films. As with all of the examples offered so far in this chapter, these are illustrative and provocative starting points rather than verdicts. A close reading of, for example, *La Marseillaise* (1938) and *Mother India* (1957) would no doubt bring to the fore textual details that cannot be explained away by these general characterisations of national cinema; but such readings could nevertheless consider the industrial practices and conditions which informed those films, and which might well have their own environmental dimension.

Japan

In order to develop a more sustained argument for the validity of an environmental approach to national cinema, I have chosen to focus on Japan. In the preface to his seminal study, *To the Distant Observer: Form and Meaning in the Japanese Cinema*, Noël Burch declares it 'beyond doubt that Japan's singular history, informed by a unique combination of forces and circumstances, has produced a cinema which is *in essence* unlike that of any other nation' (1979: 11), and although our access to, and knowledge of, global cinemas has developed considerably since Burch wrote this, it is hard to deny the thrust of his claim. As he himself notes, the self-sufficiency of Japan's film infrastructure in the early twentieth century allowed it to resist the tidal-wave influence of American and European practices which swept across so much of the world (1979: 27–8). But while Burch conceives of 'forces and circumstances' primarily in formal, cultural and industrial terms, I will look to emphasise the raw material of Japan's natural environment as a key point of reference and influence in its cinema.

Japan is an island nation; not only does it have no land borders, but it consists of a huge number of islands. These are situated off the eastern edge (downwind) of the gigantic Eurasian landmass, an arrangement which helps to determine Japan's meteorological extremities. The country's physical geography is dominated by forested mountains (which in fact feature relatively infrequently in Japanese cinema), and so populations have largely been limited to coastal areas; likewise, a shortage of farmland has made it necessary to cultivate mountain-sides for the establishment of rice paddies on terraced slopes. In *The Language of Landscape* (1998), Anne Whiston Spirn suggests that Japan's intricate land management conveys a 'false sense of control' (1998: 135), and there is certainly a precarious quality to physical conditions across the nation – something which was cruelly exposed to extreme lengths in the earthquake and tsunami of 2011. This is all complemented by regular and significant precipitation, as well as dramatic seasonal transitions (for example, Shigehiko Hasumi's writing on weather in the films of Yasujiro Ozu; see Chapter 1).

Few environmental customs from anywhere in the world are as globally recognisable as the annual spread of cherry blossom across the Japanese archipelago, and its associated celebrations – but this is only the most spectacular of a great many ways in which seasonality in Japan is a formative phenomenon. Haruo Shirane has written of Japan's 'culture of the four seasons', exploring the crucial influence that meteorological cycles have had on Japanese art and literature; but though the country's climate is the root cause of this, Shirane is careful to point out that creative artworks have tended to shape – rather than simply echo – Japan's environmental self-awareness: 'the oft-mentioned Japanese "harmony" with nature is not an inherent closeness to primary nature due to topography and climate, but a result of close ties to secondary nature' such as 'poetry, screen paintings, gardens, flower arrangement, and the tea ceremony' (2012: 18). These modes, according to Shirane, have disproportionately emphasised the transitional seasons of Spring and Autumn (because of their visual interest and poignant poetic associations), generating a cultural tradition which is both rooted in – and subtly distortive of – the Japanese environment.

From the haiku of Matsuo Basho to Akira Kurosawa's *Shichinin no Samurai* (*Seven Samurai*, 1954), and from domestic architecture to polite conversation, seasonal climates can be said to 'hang over' Japanese culture as a frame through which the natural world is often experienced and represented. Is this, as is often claimed, indicative of a cultural attitude towards, and acceptance of, ephemerality more generally? (It is interesting to note that Japan has comparatively little in the way of rivers, a natural feature which in other contexts – the poetry of Goethe, the films of Renoir – is so often understood as a material manifestation of time passing.) An engagement with the fleeting present is one of the characteristics of wabi-sabi, 'the most conspicuous and characteristic feature of what we think of as traditional Japanese beauty' (Koren 2008: 21). Wabi-sabi is a notoriously difficult idea to define, but is perhaps most usefully thought of being both an aesthetic mode and a worldview – a translation of Chinese Buddhist ideas into Japanese culture, in which simplicity, impermanence and intuition represent higher ideals than sophistication and resilience. It is, in short, not a cultural outlook attuned to the sublimity and force we often find in Western representations of natural beauty and wonder.

And yet Japan's most famous geographical feature is of course Mount Fuji, the nation's highest mountain and a subject which is *anything but* fleeting. It is surely telling, though, that Katsushika Hokusai's globally iconic series of prints, 'Thirty-Six Views of Mount Fuji', treats the mountain not only as a monumental and magisterial 'thing', but as something that can be glimpsed behind or alongside or above all manner of momentary human experiences; of work, play, danger, luxury, building, dwelling, transit, etc. To some extent this is a question of practicality – Mount Fuji is visible from Tokyo, and so is more easily integrated into social experiences than spectacular natural landmarks in other countries. But there is also something of a cultural logic at play here, too. Augustin Berque (1997) argues that Japanese environmental poetics tends not to operate according to the civilisation/wilderness binary we find in many other cultures, and that it instead offers a more gradated (and more circular) manner of perceiving the natural world. As part of his 'chorology' of Japanese eco-aesthetics, Berque posits the mountain and the ocean as non-human, divine sites which bookend the human realm; but he also stresses that these are permeable, and that religion and art in Japan have made considerable room for liminal spaces such as shorelines and rocky boundaries, allowing 'a constant toing and froing from one realm to the other' (1997: 56) – a quality which is crucial to the three Japanese films explored in this chapter.

Berque concedes that a sensitive responsiveness to natural conditions is by no means distinctive to Japanese culture (citing Rousseau and Thoreau as writers who exemplified this in a Western context), but insists that we should look for 'the singularity of forms of expression of this need according to different milieux' (1997: 67). With recourse to a remarkable metaphor, Berque complains that culture is too often conceived of as a 'hot-air balloon' untethered to a particular place, and that we should remain mindful of the 'geomorphological traits' which inform and underpin a culture's artistic practice (ibid.). This is what I intend to do in my responses to three Japanese films.

Hadaka no shima (*The Naked Island*, 1960), *Kamigami no Fukaki Yokubo* (*Profound Desires of the Gods*, 1968) and *Futatsume no mado* (*Still the Water*, 2014) are all films whose narratives are almost entirely bound to an island setting. They explore the dramatic and aesthetic affordances of such restrictions in very different ways, and although they can certainly not be said to share a coherent message or vision relating to national identity, their Japaneseness matters to their meaning in no small part because of their setting. Considering the country's topography, for a Japanese filmmaker to opt for such a setting constitutes at the very least a flirtation with metaphor, and with a national-commentary register. It also lends itself, as I hope will become clear, to a more intensified study of human/non-human dynamics.

These are not obscure films, but neither do they sit at the heart of the canon of Japanese cinema, at least as it has developed in English-language film culture. Were we to focus on this canon, the films of Yasujiro Ozu, Kenji Mizoguchi and Akira Kurosawa would certainly repay sustained ecocritical study. (Tim Palmer has proposed that the far-flung success of this triumvirate in the 1950s was partly attributable to a 'garden aesthetic, representing Japan as a source of natural abundance, beautiful and untarnished wilderness, a limitless milieu of diverse organic splendor' (2010: 212), but this takes little account of anything distinctive to Japanese conditions). The dangers of confusing a national cinema with its most critically feted auteurs are well known, and in the current study it would certainly distract from the effort to prioritise a common milieu rather than a consistent authorial vision. The island-setting criteria is rudimentary, but it will also work as an invitation to readers to cast their thoughts towards other contrasting and complementary examples, whether these be from a Japanese context – *Godjira* (*Godzilla*, 1954), *Setouchi Shonen Yakyu-dan* (*MacArthur's Children*, 1984), *Batoru Rowaiaru* (*Battle Royale*, 2000), *Oku no hito* (*The Tale of Iya*, 2013) – or indeed from further afield.

The Naked Island

Kaneto Shindo's *The Naked Island* was produced independently of the Japanese studio system, directed by a native of Hiroshima, and shot on an uninhabited island in Japan's inland sea. The film features no names of people or places, virtually no dialogue, and a story whose significant developments can be counted on the fingers of one hand. A woman, a man and their two young sons live at subsistence level on a small island, which they farm using freshwater laboriously transported by boat; the woman accidentally spills water, and is punished by the man with a brutal slap; the children catch a fish, which is sold, funding a rare restaurant meal; one son dies from a fever; the woman deliberately spills a bucket of water in a fit of despair. The repetitiveness of much of the action and the film's apparent disinterest in plot has led some to characterise *The Naked Island* as a kind of quasi-documentary, but the deliberate vague-

Fig. 14: A strongly grounded fable: *The Naked Island* (1960)

ness of its time, place and population also gives the film a strong fabular quality. This is not a fable with a strong message, though, so much as a strong grounding; the geographical location may be anonymous, but its island status could not be more potent as a force governing the film's movements and rhythms.

The actions of the two adults are largely dictated by the need to transport and distribute water, and a considerable proportion of *The Naked Island* consists of tasks leading up to, during, or immediately following the collection of freshwater from a nearby 'mainland' (which may in fact be a larger, more developed island). One of the quiet ironies in the film is the fact that the family's absolute isolation requires them to journey constantly between their island and elsewhere. The careful manoeuvring of buckets of water by boat is treated by the film as both noble and absurd. Yes, the task is carried out with extraordinary resilience, but is there perhaps vanity here as well as hardship? What motivates a people to insist on such *unnatural* isolation? The 'source' of the water from which the woman collects her supply appears to be a manmade roadside stream, perhaps part of an irrigation network; what are we to make of this disconnect between extreme labour and agricultural convenience? In 'Desert Islands', Gilles Deleuze reflects on the philosophical and creative function of islands, and in particular their ability to enable thoughts of separation and primal (re)creation: 'islands are either from before or for after humankind,' he writes (2004: 9), and *The Naked Island* bears this out in a very practical sense; the family's attempts to dwell on or with the island seems destined for failure or compromise. The experience is all labour, and virtually no fruit.

This is true of the family's agricultural efforts, but also true of what we might call their human, or humanist, experience. The limited opportunity for varied experience on the island, and the mortal need to spend time and energy collecting water, seems to have left the characters with no reserve for imaginative, playful or creative engagements with their environment – at least none to which the film grants us access. As Vernon Young wrote in a review shortly after the film's American release, 'the burden of expression' falls on the 'plastic commerce of the tides, the light and shadow, wind and rain, animal and bird life' (1963: 258). The absence of dialogue in the film is striking, but perhaps not quite so unnerving as the fact that the islanders do not (or cannot?) look around them – in recognition of one or another or

Fig. 15: Looking inwards and downwards: *The Naked Island* (1960)

of the striking landscape and seascape around them – in a non-utilitarian way. Almost every glance in the film seems to be toward the ground or into the near distance, and related to a task at hand. Shindo's tendency to use repeated framings of actions (the steering of the boat, the watering of potato crops) adds to the stultifying nature of this, as if the film is confirming a regime of patterned and purposeful looking whose constraints are dictated by the islanders' working life.

If there is an exception to this, it comes by way of the children rather than their parents. At the film's half-way point, and while their parents are delivering harvested wheat, the brothers work together to catch a large fish; the younger boy is fishing alone, but fetches his older brother to help him wrestle it safely to shore. They preserve the (still living) fish in a small rock pool, and proudly display it to their delighted parents. Despite its obvious potential as a food source for the family, fishing had not been established by the film as part of the survival routine, and so this sequence has an element of surprise and improvisation which is absent from those scenes chronicling the work of the mother and father; it is something of a transgression of the film's dramatic rhythm. One cannot quite imagine the parents catching the fish, so ingrained have they become in a particular system of working with their surroundings. Their delight at its capture prompts the only gesture of happiness we see in *The Naked Island*, as the father congratulates his youngest son by plunging him into the water. But even this action will have a tragic echo or variation later on in the film, when the older brother is ceremoniously buried at the island's peak.

To the extent that Shindo's film is an account of life on an island in challenging conditions, it is often dispiriting, and keeps a surprisingly cool, almost unfeeling distance from its own protagonists. But as an exercise in film form, and as an attempt to render island living through moving images, *The Naked Island* is extremely inventive. The film's deployment of montage is particularly striking, not least because we would probably imagine the labourious processes which are so vital to the film as ripe for treatment in sequence shots – for example, a long take disembarking from the boat *with* the woman, and travelling alongside her as she carefully struggles up the slope to the farmland. Instead, the camera tends to be stationary, and positioned so as to anticipate the (all too predictable) movement of bodies around the island, and to frame them accordingly. The film also overlaps one task with another, so there is rarely the pleasing arc of an activity which has begun and ended in one sequence. Just as the characters themselves never rest between activities, the film's shot-to-shot relations generate a sort of restlessness or incompleteness. For example, when the man and woman come to harvest their wheat, a close up of the woman scything cuts to a low-angle shot of her lifting a sheaf; moments later, a tilt downwards reveals that she is now removing the wheat heads; a few seconds subsequently, the two of them are now threshing the wheat with flails. These different tasks are not interspersed with visual or aural 'beats' of any kind, and in fact the melancholic score carries across the shots to support the continuity across them. There is no opportunity for repose.

When the family visit a nearby town to sell their fish, they encounter a television in a shop window, and stare at it in incomprehension. The broadcast is of a young woman in a black leotard against a blank background, performing an energetic exercise-cum-dance – an activity whose seeming pointlessness leaves the islanders bemused. It is a sequence which throws into sharp relief another important aspect of the island setting in Japanese cinema; an isolated land mass not only invokes Japan itself, but it can also dramatise with great force the tensions between modernity and pre-modernity which have been particularly fraught in twentieth-century Japan. Setting out the scope of his book on this topic, *Overcome by Modernity*, Harry D. Harootunian describes how interwar Japan was 'distinguished by a consciousness that oscillated furiously between recognizing the peril of being overcome by modernity and the impossible imperative of overcoming it' (2001: x), a dynamic which has been played out to a greater or lesser extent in many Japanese films, most famously in the work of Ozu and Mizoguchi. Until the mid-nineteenth century, Japan was in self-imposed exile from dramatic developments in global trade and industry, and although the post-war American occupation seemed to settle the question of whether or not Japan would be a 'modern' country (a strong parliament, improved rights for women, etc), the dilemma of whether to look outward or inward, forward or backward, was certainly not settled by 1960. It is virtually impossible not to map onto *The Naked Island* a schema, however reductive, of island/Japan/tradition vs. mainland/global modernity. A similar schema is taken up by Shohei Imamura in *The Profound Desires of the Gods*, but while Shindo builds from this idea an austere and ambivalent fable, Imamura offers up a carnival-cum-menagerie, and a wholly different set of responses to Japan's *islandness*.

Profound Desires of the Gods

In contrast to the 'naked island' of Shindo's film, which is palpably close to larger and more modernised habitations, the (fictional) island of Kurage in *Profound Desires of the Gods* is fundamentally removed from the Japanese mainland. Imamura's island also has a closer real-world correlative than Shindo's, namely the island of Okinawa. Part of a larger chain of islands which sits roughly between Taiwan, Japan and mainland China, Okinawa has a rather ambiguous and ambivalent relationship to Japanese nationhood; deeply influenced by other South Asian cultural traditions, it also remained under American control through to the 1970s, and occupies something of a playground status in the Japanese cultural imagination.

A social and geographical outlier, Okinawa was perhaps an inevitable subject for Shohei Imamura, a director drawn to the margins of a (Japanese) society whose pretensions of purity he consistently took issue with. In an overview of Imamura's filmmaking character and career, Donald Richie suggests that, throughout his work, 'naturalness – hidden, muffled, concealed though it is by official Japan [...] is irrepressible' (1997: 8). Richie is here using 'natural' to describe a certain manner of human behaviour – 'selfish, lusty, amoral, innocent' (ibid.) – but is also referring to the preponderance of animal life which is shown and alluded to in Imamura's films, and which parallels and contextualises the films'

human drama. The director of *Buta to gunkan* (*Pigs and Battleships*, 1961) and *Nippon Konchuki* (*The Insect Woman*, 1963) made films about people whose instincts and gestures were as biological as they were social. *Profound Desires of the Gods* is firmly in this mode, but here the meditation on nature and naturalness is given a special focus and inflection by dint of the island setting.

Kurage is home to a rather disorienting mix of religious rituals, superstition, feudal working conditions and vibrant wildlife. It is paradisal and deeply dysfunctional, and the film posits the Futori family as a kind of symptom of the island's extraordinary character. The Futoris are overseen by the incestuous Yamamori (Kanjuro Arashi), father *and* grandfather to Toriko (Hideko Okiyama), a mentally unstable and sexually voracious woman who is also believed to have shamanistic powers. Yamamori's son Nekichi (Rentaro Mikuni) spends much of the film in a giant hole in the ground, trying to dislodge a huge boulder which is said to have blown onto the island as divine retribution for his own sexual transgressions (he is in love with his sister). Into this steps Kariya (Kazuo Kitamura), an engineer dispatched by his Tokyo-based sugar-manufacturer employer to research the water supply on Kurage, and who hires Nekichi's son Kametaro (Choichiro Kawarasaki) as an assistant. Imamura intersperses the ensuing drama with quasi-documentary sequences giving voice to the island's politically disenfranchised and economically frustrated youth, as well as songs by a wheelchair-bound minstrel recounting the origin myth of Kurage – a story which is itself founded on incest, and which bears a strong resemblance to Japan's own creation story.

The Futori family is maligned by other islanders for its 'beastliness', but as far as Imamura's worldview goes, this is hardly a damning quality. Nekichi's and Toriko's closeness to animal life – their physically instinctive actions as well as their tendency to handle living creatures – is neither celebrated nor mocked by the film, which (like *The Naked Island*) does not adopt the affective point of view of anyone on or beyond the island. We never look at the family *with* a character about whom we know or care, and nowhere in *Profound Desires* is there a normative rhythm or set of relations against which the Futoris' character can be judged. Early on in the film, immediately after its opening credits, a short anecdotal sequence depicts a group of Kurage fisherman passing by a larger commercial vessel carrying sleeping pigs; one of the pigs falls overboard, and is quickly devoured by a shark. Is this aberrant? Symbolic? Foreboding? Natural? The scene establishes the fact that Kurage as an island and *Profound Desires of the Gods* as a film are not best understood according to notions of ecological harmony and permanence (of the kind we might associate with Japanese Shintoism or wabi-sabi aesthetics), but rather of instinct and collision. This is an ecosystem whose logic we have little hope of understanding; it is also one which includes the fisherman and the boats on which they travel, just as it will include the dynamite with which Nekichi conducts his own fishing, and the trains and aeroplanes which eventually arrive at the island. In most films these developments would surely function as disturbances or violent impositions, but *Profound Desires of the Gods* is careful to disassociate the image of the island from the idea of equilibrium. The natural order of Kurage – its palpable 'sense of completeness' (Mellen 1976: 386) – is deep and unpredictable disorder.

Which is not to say that the film's narrative is chaotic or unstructured. The arrival of Kariya, or 'Mr. Engineer' as he is sometimes called, provides a familiar and predictable storytelling motif to complement and counterbalance the sheer oddness of much of what we encounter. The unwelcome visiting expert is a type who often features in films about 'off-the-grid' communities, such as *Wild River* (1960) and *Local Hero* (discussed in Chapter 2), and it is common for his or her initial utilitarianism to be compromised or undermined by the emotional and sensorial experiences provided by the new environment. This is true of Kariya, who is initially impatient to locate a water source on Kurage as soon as possible, in order that he might escape its stifling heat and its bothersome wildlife – but by the film's halfway point has been seduced by Toriko, and lies half-dressed sprawling on the sunlit beach (his spectacles discarded on a nearby rock), being hand-fed molluscs direct from the ocean.

Fig. 17: The visiting
expert 'goes native':
*Profound Desires of
the Gods* (1968)

And yet this almost cartoonish characterisation of the modern main-lander 'going native' belies a more subtle strategy on the part of *Profound Desires of the Gods*, whereby the engineer's expedition is positioned *not* as an invasion or a contamination of Kurage's wellbeing to be triumphantly foiled by the island's charm, but as something which could demonstrably improve the lives of many islanders. A number of throwaway references are made to Kurage's unbearably salty drinking water, and the one pre-cious freshwater source which is being hid from the engineer (by Ryu (Yoshi Katô), who effectively manages the island) is likewise being denied to the majority of Kurage inhabitants. Looked at from one perspective, the engineer's mission is a culturally insensitive imposition of modern tech-nology, which leads inexorably to the opening up of Kurage by way of a new airport; but his exploration is also born out of a concern for, and expertise in, the physical conditions and capacities of the island, an island whose resources are being palpably misdirected in service of a religious tradition which is no more 'natural' than industrial sugar production. To suggest, as Mika Ko (2013: 83) does, that the film indulges 'Japan's nostalgia for a utopian vision of its own pre-modernity' is surely to simplify its extraordi-narily complex meditation on purity and impurity, regression and progress.

Profound Desires of the Gods climaxes with the ritual assassination of Nekichi and his sister-cum-lover Uma (Yasuko Matsui) as they attempt to escape Kurage, a killing carried out by a group which includes Nekichi's son, Kametaro. An epilogue then shows us the island five years later, after an airport and train line have been established there; Kariya is visiting with his wife and mother-in-law, and during a sight-seeing train tour they are shown 'Toriko Rock', a huge statue-like formation on the coastline, which – according to local legend – formed when a woman was waiting for her lover to return. The lover for whom Toriko was waiting was Kariya

Fig. 18: Catching a glimpse of Toriko Rock: *Profound Desires of the Gods* (1968)

himself, and logically speaking this 'legend' could only be a few years old. What do we make of it? The rock, as far as we can see (through the fleeting and obstructed telephoto composition) does indeed resemble a seated woman, but nothing in the film's presentation bestows on it any special status of the kind we might expect for such a miraculous, uncanny manifestation. Perhaps it has always been on the island, and some local people mischievously applied the myth as testament to an entertaining local scandal. The attempt by Kariya to dismiss the story as an example of the islanders' delightfully primitive naivety does not quite convince us; after all, the film has shown us only minutes before Toriko sitting on a rocky beach gazing longingly out towards the sea, and has previously given credence to the claim that she has supernatural faculties.

Perhaps the rock is just a rock, but it sits on the edge of an island which has nurtured ideas of animism and ecological agency that cannot be easily dismissed. Imamura approaches the island and its inhabitants in such a way that leaves room for those ideas without romantically indulging them. His film presents Kurage as a meeting point between the instincts of a pre-modern Japan and the priorities of a rapidly modernising nation state, but the contrast is muddied. It is not clear which of these worldviews has a stronger attachment to the sentience of Toriko's Rock. And neither is it clear whether we have watched a film about an island on the periphery of Japanese culture, or one at its heart.

Still the Water

Each of the Japanese films discussed in this chapter develops a narrative and aesthetic account of what it means to live on an island. In both *The Naked Island* and *Profound Desires of the Gods*, the condition of being geographically and socially separate (and separated?), a condition which cannot help but implicitly address ideas of Japanese nationhood, has traumatic currency. The apartness of an island, rather than facilitating self-sufficiency and harmony, in these films places seemingly irresolvable strains and pressures on human and natural resources. Naomi Kawase's *Still the Water* also features something of this tension between the centripetal and centrifugal forces of island living, between a profound sensitivity to local circumstances and a disquieting concern for what lies beyond those circumstances, but it tends to emphasise the restorative and revelatory potential of the island environment.

Another way of putting this would be to say that, of the three films, *Still the Water* is the least concerned with the profound compromises that island conditions can impose. The monotony which underpins *The Naked Island*, for example, or the siege mentality of the Kurage community in *Profound Desires of the Gods*, are absent. This is a film in which islanders treat their locale as an opportunity for spiritual reflection and projection (of the kind which would be inconceivable in *The Naked Island* and *Profound Desires of the Gods*), and a number of reviewers have in fact responded with some exasperation to the film's rather saccharine conjoining of personal, ecological and religious ideals. Maggie Lee in *Variety* accuses Kawase of 'padding her modest human drama with pretentious yet hollow musings', and takes issue with the 'nature worship and pompous philosophising' on the part of the film and its characters alike (2014). I too have reservations about the film's rhetoric, but nevertheless find it to be another revealing example of what happens when an island setting becomes a clear and guiding influence on the style and meaning of a Japanese film.

On the shores of Amami-Oshima, an island about two hundred miles northeast of Okinawa, a teenage boy, Kaito (Nijiro Murakami), finds a dead body which has been washed up by a violent storm. Rather than concern itself with the identification of, and explanation for, the dead man, *Still the Water* focuses mainly on Kaito and his on/off girlfriend Kyoko (Jun Yoshinaga) as they simultaneously navigate their adolescent love and their coming to terms with family trauma (his parents have separated, and her mother is dying of an incurable illness).

One important, but implicit, consequence of the corpse, and Kaito's discovery of it, is that it entrenches Kaito's distrust of the ocean, a distrust which becomes an important thread in the film. Kaito's reluctance to swim

Fig. 19: Young lovers and their geography: *Still the Water* (2014)

in the water is developed in sharp contrast to Kyoko's supreme ease and confidence (in a rather surreal sequence, she swims fully clothed underwater), and the film clearly invites us to see this in relation to their capacity for emotional sensitivity; Kaito is painfully uncommunicative with his mother, and his self-pity impedes his ability to empathise with her, while Kyoko accepts her own mother's mortality, and has an almost miraculous capacity for 'processing' her family's situation in terms of mutability rather than tragedy. The final scene of *Still the Water* shows the two teenagers swimming together underwater, naked and holding hands, a rather neat conclusion to the film's 'taking-the-plunge' metaphor, and perhaps the most vivid example of what critics such as Lee recoiled from – an all-too-convenient marriage of natural splendour, individual humility and philosophical awakening.

The opening shots of *Still the Water* form a rhetorical prologue. Long-distance landscape shots of an increasingly turbulent storm and large waves breaking upon a shore are followed by a cut and a short blackout; a final establishing shot then shows the same stretch of beach in serene stillness. The rhythm of the cutting and the quality of the light suggest that the calm shortly follows the storm – dawn the next day, we would guess – and this could be interpreted, on a rather schematic level, as indicative of Kawase's tendency to regard tranquility as a state to which things will reliably and eternally return (although second-time viewers of the film will be alive to the irony that a dead body floats within or nearby this scenic arrangement). More significant than the 'message' of this passage, though, is the fact that it establishes a particular mode of looking at the environment, especially the ocean, one whose characteristics will recur throughout the film.

Firstly, it is a *looking out*; with very few exceptions, *Still the Water* is a film which imagines the island habitat from the inside out, inviting us to look with, rather than at, the islanders and their home. Secondly, the opening shots are not attributed to a character, but the fact that they register a time lapse between 'storm' and 'calm' gives them a roughly *subjective* quality; the film has no fewer than fifteen shots of the ocean which, like these, cannot be described as point-of-view shots, but whose cumulative effect is nevertheless that of a consciousness being drawn out to sea. And thirdly, the sequence is unashamedly *choreographed*; nowhere in *Still the Water* does Kawase really try to evoke the irregularity or unpredictability which some artists (and audiences) might believe to be vitally constitutive of 'naturalness'. Her camera is never caught off guard by actions or details for which it was unprepared, and although only a small number of shots have a markedly omniscient quality to them (including a remarkable aerial shot which traces, presumably from an aeroplane, the contours of an underwater ridge through translucent ocean water), the island and its actions are regarded throughout the film from a position of knowing detachment.

Taken together, tendencies such as these position *Still the Water* not as a study of the island, or a documentary record whose production has had to contend with the challenges of a pro-filmic world, but rather as an impressionistic account whose sensibility – of contented resignation – is very close to that of Kyoko and her family. Kyoko's dying mother, Isa (Miyuki Matsuda), is a shaman, and is able to share with her husband, Toru (Tetta Sugimoto), and daughter an acceptance of the transience of human life. She describes herself as being on the 'threshold' between gods and humans, and therefore undisturbed by the prospect of moving from mortal life to the afterlife. Returning from hospital to the family home for her final days, Isa sits with Kyoko and Toru on the threshold between the inside and outside of their house, which we learn has been a favourite spot of hers for many years. Before long, Isa stands up and moves towards a huge banyan tree, as if magnetically drawn into its field. Toru reassures Kyoko that her mother probably 'sees something' that others are unable to. But what do *we* see? The film cuts to a shot of Isa and the tree from a position some distance away from the house, as if to declare our access to be more far-reaching than Toru or Kyoko's – but all we see is Isa place her hand upon the trunk, hold on to a branch, and look out to sea. As is the case in many sequences throughout *Still the Water*, the natural environment is venerated, but through the filter of a religious impulse which longs for the invisible and the otherworldly. Richie argues that Shohei Imamura 'never asks us to believe anything we are not shown' (1997: 22); Kawase, by contrast, shows us a rich material and atmospheric world while seeming unconvinced by its inherent, substantial importance.

When Isa looks out to sea, a cut to an extreme long shot of the water is *not* confirmed as a point-of-view shot, and so remains somewhat suspended in its meaning and function – as are many similar shots throughout *Still the Water*. But such shots are not arbitrary and, as already suggested, they could be said to be closely attuned to the (non-individualised) experience of island inhabitants. (After all, for those who live on Amami-Oshima, looking out to sea is a fact of life, and not necessarily the exceptional personal experience it is for others – such as Antoine Doinel at the end of *Les quatre cent coups* (see Chapter 1)). These images are most fully integrated into the film's drama during an important scene shared between Kyoko and Keito, during which the two teenagers sit together on a bench overlooking the sea; the sun is setting, and its glow casts a warm light across their faces. It certainly *looks* like a romantic set piece, and the scene does indeed culminate in a kiss, but Kyoko and Keito arrive at this by way of a conversation about the sea that separates them as much as it unites them.

Following an initially tense exchange about Keito's knowledge (which he denies) of the dead body, Kyoko challenges him about his relationship to the water, which she seems to believe is related to his emotional and sexual reticence:

Kyoko: Why don't you try surfing? My father said you should get
    into the sea.
Keito: The sea is scary.
Kyoko: Huh?
Keito: The sea … it's alive.
Kyoko: I'm alive too.
[pause]
Kyoko: My father told me, when you're surfing – he's only felt this

Fig. 20: Taking the plunge: *Still the Water* (2014)

> rarely – but there are moments when you feel like you become
> one with the sea.
> *Keito*: It's way too big for that.
> *Kyoko*: [ignoring Keito] I thought that's like sex.

Most of this exchange takes the form of a two-shot in profile, in which
Keito is closer to the camera but Kyoko's face is clearer to us. When she
begins to report her father's thoughts on surfing, the film cuts to a shot
of the sea – yet another 'loose' point-of-view shot, only this time there
is something narratively at stake, namely the dilemma of whether to
regard the sea as an enticing opportunity for spiritual enlargement, or as
a force whose vastness and unknowability are terrifying. (Fiona Handyside
writes that beaches can bring to a film's narrative 'too much meaning, an
excess of meaningful potential' (2014: 7).) We know that both characters
are bringing their own experiences and desires to bear on the water, and
the image neither proves nor disproves either compulsion. How could it?
Because this is a film, the sea appears in the form of a framed, fleeting
moving image; not an illustration of the abstract 'sea' about which Kyoko
and Keito talk, but rather a tiny proportion of that millennia-old sea's surface at one moment, a little under twenty seconds. To this extent we could
consider it an *inadequate* image, but this is surely what the scene has set
out to explore – how human thoughts and feelings take shape in dialogue
with an environment whose complexity and magnitude always lie beyond
comprehension.

Still the Water is perhaps a little too sure of nature's therapeutic potential, too confident that the non-human world can be engaged with in such
a way that resolves unease. Towards the film's end, Toru talks to Keito and
Kyoko about his love of surfing and his mourning for Isa, comparing his
departed wife with a wave whose energy continually sustains him, imply-
ing that it is this attitude which has allowed him to grieve with such for-
bearance and peace. Considering that Toru seems to have lived his life in
conditions which have allowed him to acquire such an outlook, this seems
to be a rather exclusive and rarefied sentiment. Which is why it is important for the film that these words are addressed primarily to Keito, a young
man who has only recently come to Amami-Oshima, and whose efforts to
understand its environment and its values have caused no small amount
of anguish. *Still the Water* certainly aligns itself with Toru's worldview, but
Keito's presence counterbalances this; Kawase knows that the island is
the seed bed for ways of thinking and being that are only 'natural' on a
local scale.

CONCLUSION

Throughout this book, I have attempted to elucidate a way of exploring film texts which takes full account of the medium's ability to engage with non-human, environmental, 'natural' subject matter. A fundamental challenge for ecocritical writing of any kind is that of finding a balance between the craft of a particular work and the irreducibility of the world to which it refers. In trying to meet this challenge, I have been led to focus largely on films which themselves achieve such a balance, which acknowledge something of the world's totality without disavowing their creative and expressive ambitions.

Although the films discussed do, I believe, engage the natural environment with deliberate care and considerable imagination, none of them can really be considered 'green' film texts; theirs is not an environmentalist rhetoric. My approach has, though, been an ethical one, to the extent that it has encouraged readers to maintain an alertness to the natural world as something which cannot be understood simply as setting or theme. Films are never categorically 'environmental' any more than we are, but they can – like us – develop a rich and multifaceted relationship with their environment, not least by reminding us that such relationships are a matter of both perception and physical circumstance. 'We are aware of the world,' writes Arthur C. Danto, 'yet seldom aware, if at all, of the special way in which we are aware of the world' (2001: 231). Narrative cinema can help us better understand this awareness, allowing us simultaneous access to records of the world *and* the creative consciousness through which the recording takes place.

I have tried to make the case that such 'awareness' does not simply boil down to the overt emphasis a film places on nature; what is at stake is not how much screen time is given to flowers and rivers and mountains, but the *kind* of significance and meanings such phenomena accrue over the course of a film – what we could call the *nature* of their presence in the work. And even if a narrative film can only show us these phenomena in relatively fleeting moments, and as relatively superficial surfaces, such 'glances' can have extraordinary potential. 'In their capacity to set forth the figure and texture of any given occupant of any given environment,' writes Edward S. Casey, 'surfaces act as sheaves for that environment, showing and specifying what would otherwise be mere perceptual flotsam and jetsam' (2003: 196). Casey writes this in the context of an argument he makes (drawing on the ideas of Emmanuel Levinas) for the ethical currency of the glance in the emergence and maintenance of an environmental awareness. Rather than disparage surface details as superficial, Casey argues, we should value them precisely because of their expressivity and simplicity; we should trust our *perception* of the environment as a vital starting point for journeys towards greater ecological responsiveness.

A recurrent theme throughout this book has been the importance of point of view and perception in the study of a film's engagement with the natural environment; the need of attending to environmental views and relations *within* the world of the film – such as those of George Loomis in *Niagara* or Verónica in *La mujer sin cabeza* – if one is to develop an account of the film's own environmental character. This is, I think, a fruitful approach, and one which is somewhat underexplored in ecocritical film studies. But I would like to conclude by once again broadening out the coverage of my discussion, by returning to the theme of Chapter 1 (namely the environmental subtext across many areas of film studies), and by bringing together a range of dissimilar passages of writing which all, nevertheless, combine close attention to a film's environmentality with broad and complex issues. Taken together, the words and ideas of these contemporary writers go further than I have had the opportunity to in the main chapters of this book to demonstrate the sheer breadth of environmental film study – each in their own way registering a film's sustained *glance* as a call to think about the natural world, and about what we make of it.

Michael Wood on movement

In *Film: A Very Short Introduction* (2012b), Michael Wood 'sets the scene' for his reflective study of the medium by way of a hypothetical response to an unassuming sequence:

> A man stands before a grave in a country cemetery. He doesn't move, nothing moves; no birds, a still world. But this is a man in a motion picture, we have seen him move, and he will move again in a moment when his spell of meditation and memory is over. The film in John Ford's *Young Mr. Lincoln* (1939). The man is Henry Fonda playing a grieving Lincoln as he lingers over Ann Rutledge's grave.
>
> You like the shot and its framing, so you pause the film. Now it looks and feels quite different. How can it? What could the difference between a stilled and a moving picture of a scene where there is no movement? You start the film again, and pause it again. Yes, quite different. Then you realise. There is a river at the back of the image, and in the motion picture it flows, there are pieces of ice drifting down the dark surface. (2012: 1)

There is in this thought experiment only implicit attention to film craft (performance, cinematography, mise-en-scène, etc). Wood's primary emphasis is instead on the fact of *encounter* between a film and a viewer – a viewer not only accustomed to laws of nature, but accustomed to laws of nature as they tend to be employed in narrative film. As he sees it, the physical environment in a scene such as this is not only a formal and narrative constituent; it is the very contract between film and viewer that this story is happening in a world whose time is 'real'. 'If nothing else moves in *Young Mr. Lincoln*,' Wood continues, 'the water in the river does; and if the water doesn't move, it isn't a movie' (2012: 2).

One way of characterising ecocritical film studies would be to say that it is the pursuit of other instances in which a film's very ability to communicate its information and achieve its most meaningful sensorial effects is one and the same with its particular treatment of the natural environment. Wood playfully conflates the criteria for what constitutes *a* film with what constitutes *this* film. Of course not all films require moving rivers, but it is an illuminating question to ask of other work: which features of an environment become the assurance of a film narrative having taken place in the world?

Slavoj Žižek on metaphor

Adrian Ivakhiv takes Tarkovsky's *Stalker* to be a work in which we can see with particular vividness how films traffic in material, social and perceptual ecologies (2013: 1–29). Slavoj Žižek's approach to the film (and one which Ivakhiv incorporates into his own model) is more focused on its psychoanalytical register than its environmental qualities, but he is nevertheless acutely aware of the 'typical Tarkovskian landscape', defined as 'the human environment in decay reclaimed by nature' (1990: 227), and which in *Stalker* determines the form of 'the zone'.

What is especially distinctive about Žižek's response to the film is his claim that a particular political-historical point of reception will have determined (or heavily influenced) the range of meanings an audience could project onto *Stalker*:

> For an ex-citizen of the defunct Soviet Union, the notion of a forbidden zone gives rise to (at least) five associations: the Zone is (1) Gulag, i.e. a separated prison territory; (2) a territory poisoned or otherwise rendered uninhabitable by some technological (bio-chemical, nuclear...) catastrophe, like Chernobyl; (3) the secluded domain in which the *nomenklatura* lives; (4) foreign territory to which access is prohibited (like the enclosed West Berlin in the midst of the GDR); (5) a territory where a meteorite struck (like Tunguska in Siberia). The point, of course, is that the question 'So which is the true meaning of the Zone?' is false and misleading: the very indeterminacy of what lies beyond the limit is primary, and different positive contents fill in this preceding gap. (Ibid.)

Not all of these historically informed associations would have been 'in play' at the time of the film's production (*Stalker*, it can be easy to forget, predates the Chernobyl disaster). But neither can we go far as to say that any filmed landscape will be a 'blank slate' onto which a viewer will project his or her own cultural and environmental associations, regardless of their historical or geographical connection to the film. Žižek's list, I think, is both a testament to the openness and profundity of *Stalker*, and a reminder that certain historically informed interpretations nevertheless force the issue. Faced with extraordinary but ambiguous film landscapes, we cannot simply accept their 'indeterminacy'; there will almost always be 'positive contents', limits on the universality of a filmed world.

Salma Monani and Matthew Beehr on social justice

The temptation to separate off non-human landscapes as sites of ideological neutrality and innocence is widespread, and is often hard to resist. For many, this is the very definition of nature; a de-politicised and non-cultural balm, a 'separate, timeless, wild sphere' (McKibben 2003: 47). But it is not a definition which bears much scrutiny, and there is no starker illustration of the irregularity of environmental meaning – of the fact that 'green aesthetics' can never be a universal value system – than agricultural slavery and servitude. Human history has seen millions of people forcibly conditioned to labour on and with environments, people who have simply not been able to find in wild spaces and far-reaching vistas promises of escape, redemption, exultation or stimulation. As Salma Monani and Matthew Beehr write of a character in John Sayles' *Honeydripper* (2007), a film set in the cotton fields of 1950s Alabama, 'with his arrival in the fields being the result of injustice, it would be hard for Sonny to appreciate either his presence in this environment or the environment itself' (2011: 11).

In these terms, 'appreciation' becomes a less benign activity than it is often taken to be; what are the social conditions which have enabled a film and its characters to engage their environments in particular ways? Monani and Beehr find that *Honeydripper*, in 'its continuous careful attention to the natural environment in the context of its characters' circumstances, presents a compelling narrative of African American environmental attitudes' (2011: 6). These circumstances are determined by race relations and social inequality, in such a way that manifestly affects how African American characters in the film can interact with the landscape: 'The combination of disparate origins and lack of investment in the fields makes it difficult for the labourers there to form a community, either with each other or the extended natural world' (2011: 15). Monani and Beehr trace how Sayles actually moves towards a somewhat hopeful resolution, a positive rejoinder to widespread images of 'African Americans in toxic and polluted environments, or distanced entirely from the natural world and engaged in excessive, materialistic consumerism' (2011: 21–2). In short, while many environmental experiences – awe, disorientation, harmony, inspiration – seem to be tied to individual perception, they will invariably be influenced by social parameters such as ethnicity, age, prosperity and gender. Navigating the relationship between a film character's socialised view of nature with that of the film itself is an increasingly important challenge for ecocritical film studies.

Lucy Fife Donaldson on artificiality

Many of the analyses in this book have assumed a discernible distinction between natural and man-made environments, exploring films' special attention to, and treatment of, the former. The distinction has not always been straightforward, but it has tended to matter to the narrative and meaning of the film in question. In Lucy Fife Donaldson's writing on *Vertigo* (1958), demarcations of naturalness are shown to matter less than the textural character of various environments. Imagining the palpability of costumes and props, flora and fauna, as well as the cumulative texture of shot-to-shot relations, is for Donaldson an important part of interpreting cinema. According to her model of analysis, a film environment will always be a sensorial arrangement just as it is one of narrative, cultural or ideological meaning.

And so, in *Vertigo*, when Scottie (James Stewart) and Madeleine (Kim Novak) visit a forest and a (seemingly nearby) rocky beach, the effect is not of an 'escape to nature' in the generic sense of that term; instead, 'the material qualities of space seem to become increasingly elastic, as back projection is used interchangeably with matte paintings and interior sets in order to trouble the experience of this environment for Scottie, and for us' (2014: 91). Of course it is not incidental to the film that these famous scenes invoke monumental and pre-cultural (natural) forces, namely gigantic trees and crashing waves – but Donaldson is alive to the fact that the overriding sense is of profound surreality rather than ecological communion.

The forest in *Vertigo* is not a worldly space, 'but rather an entirely plastic one that seems to move backwards and forwards, folding in on itself and expanding between shots' (2014: 93). Alfred Hitchcock is no more taken by the majesty of the giant redwoods than is Scottie. The forest is a means to a formal, affective end, for filmmaker and film characters alike. But in her attention to those qualities of film which are perhaps the hardest to articulate – 'the depth that spills over'; 'the tangibility revealed by light and sound'; 'the feeling of a world' (2014: 48) – Donaldson convincingly demonstrates the fact realism, veracity and indexicality do not demarcate what ecocritical film writing can explore. Fabricated worlds are by no means out of bounds.

Laura Mulvey on disaster

Abbas Kiarostami's Koker triology – *Khaneh-ye Doust Kojast?* (*Where Is My Friend's House?*, 1987), *Va Zendegi Edameh Darad* (*And Life Goes On,* 1992) and *Zir-e Darakhtan-e Zeitoun* (*Through the Olive Trees,* 1994) – is perhaps the most critically acclaimed model of film realism since postwar Italian cinema. It is marked not only by a bracing immediacy and naturalism of human performance, but also by a deeply reflexive approach towards these very qualities. The textual relationships between the three films are complex and multi-layered, but the trilogy's major structuring point of reference is the Manjil–Rudbar earthquake of 1990, which struck the region in which *Where Is My Friend's House?* was shot; this disaster prompts Kiarostami to stage a semi-fictionalised return to the area in *And Life Goes On*, which in turn becomes the subject of diegetic reenactments in *Through the Olive Trees.*

Laura Mulvey, in the context of her writing about stillness and film, explores the 'earthquake's impact on Kiarostami's cinema in relation to reality and its representation,' and how it opened a gap 'separating the reality of a traumatic event and any attempt to turn it into an exegesis, a representational account of the event' (2006: 128). One of the major themes of environmental film and media studies, particularly as it relates to current and imminent ecological crises, is the sheer impossibility of showing environmental disaster in a manner that is at all adequate to the subject at hand. But rather than link Kiarostami's cinematic disaster to a contemporary moment of environmental turmoil, Mulvey (borrowing the terms of Gilles Deleuze) traces a longer and narrower trajectory back to European modernist film: 'Like the volcano in *Viaggio in Italia* (*Journey to*

Italy (1954)), 'the earthquake represents the sudden eruption into move-ment of something that should have remained still' (2006: 131).

The term 'disaster film' is usually used to designate a genre which, unlike the Koker trilogy, sets about creating and recreating a catastrophe as a narrativised event – an exegesis. Kiarostami (and Rossellini), mean-while, indicate a different line of possibility, in which the disaster is felt through its after effects, asking what it means for a worldly event to have been so profound that the very idea of stillness has become uncertain (the stakes here are not dissimilar to those in critical writing about film and Hiroshima's atomic trauma). After 1990, the filmed landscape of *Where Is My Friend's House?* ceased to be a stable ground against which human dynamics could be played out; the earth 'should have remained still', but didn't. It is difficult to imagine a more succinct summary of what it means to watch filmed environments at the onset of the Anthropocene.

FILMOGRAPHY

Non-English language films are listed here under their English-language release titles.

The 400 Blows (François Truffaut, 1959, France)
A Taste of Honey (Tony Richardson, 1961, UK)
Aftershock (Nicolás López, 2012, USA)
All That Heaven Allows (Douglas Sirk, 1955, USA)
And Life Goes On (Abbas Kiarostami, 1992, Iran)
Antichrist (Lars Von Trier, 2008, Denmark)
The Asphalt Jungle (John Huston, 1950, USA)
Barry Lyndon (Stanley Kubrick, 1975, UK/USA)
Battle Royale (Kinji Fukasaku, 2000, Japan)
The Big Combo (Joseph H. Lewis, 1955, USA)
The Big Heat (Fritz Lang, 1953, USA)
The Big Lebowski (Joel and Ethan Coen, 1998, USA)
Black Coal, Thin Ice (Diao Yinan, 2014, China)
Black God White Devil (Glauber Rocha, 1964, Brazil)
Blackboards (Samira Makhmalbaf, 2000, Iran/Italy/Japan)
Blade Runner (Ridley Scott, 1982, USA)
Blind Shaft (Li Yang, 2003, China)
Blow-Up (Michelangelo Antonioni, 1966, UK/Italy)
Brokeback Mountain (Ang Lee, 2005, USA)
Chinatown (Roman Polanski, 1974, USA)
Chungking Express (Wong Kar-wai, 1994, Hong Kong)
Citizen Kane (Orson Welles, 1941, USA)

Coup de Torchon (Bertrand Tavernier, 1981, France)

The Crazies (George A. Romero, 1973, USA)

Crouching Tiger Hidden Dragon (Ang Lee, 2000, Taiwan/Hong Kong/USA/ China)

Daisies (Věra Chytilová, 1966, Czechoslovakia)

Dark City (Alex Proyas, 1998, Australia/USA)

Daughters of the Dust (Julie Dash, 1993, USA)

Detour (Edgar G. Ulmer, 1945, USA)

The Devil Operation (Stephanie Boyd, 2010, Peru)

Die Nibelungen: Siegfried (Fritz Lang, 1924, Germany)

Earth (Alexandr Dovzhenko, 1930, Soviet Union)

El Topo (Alejandro Jodorowsky, 1970, Mexico)

Fitzcarraldo (Werner Herzog, 1982, Germany)

Force Majeure (Ruben Östlund, 2014, France/Norway/Sweden)

The General Line (Grigori Aleksandrov and Sergei Eisenstein, 1929, Soviet Union)

Godzilla (Ishiro Honda, 1954, Japan)

Gun Crazy (Joseph H. Lewis, 1950, USA)

Hannah and Her Sisters (Woody Allen, 1986, USA)

He Walked by Night (Alfred L. Werker, 1948, USA)

The Headless Woman (Lucrecia Martel, 2008, Argentina)

Hidden (Michael Haneke, 2005, France)

High Sierra (Raoul Walsh, 1941, USA)

Hiroshima mon amour (Alain Resnais, 1959, France)

Honeydripper (John Sayles, 2007, USA)

The Host (Bong Joon-ho, 2006, South Korea)

I Know Where I'm Going! (Michael Powell and Emeric Pressburger, 1945, UK)

The Insect Woman (Shohei Imamura, 1963, Japan)

It Happened One Night (Frank Capra, 1934, USA)

Journey to Italy (Roberto Rossellini, 1954, France/Italy)

Jurassic Park (Steven Spielberg, 1993, USA)

Key Largo (John Huston, 1948, USA)

Kiss Me Deadly (Robert Aldrich, 1955, USA)

L'Argent (Robert Bresson, 1983, France)

L'Atalante (Jean Vigo, 1934, France)

L'Eclisse (Michelangelo Antonioni, 1963, Italy)

La Marseillaise (Jean Renoir, 1938, France)

Late Spring (Yasujiro Ozu, 1949, Japan)
Local Hero (Bill Forsyth, 1983, UK)
London (Patrick Keiller, 1994, UK)
The Long Goodbye (Robert Altman, 1973, USA)
MacArthur's Children (Masahiro Shinoda, 1984, Japan)
Manhattan (Woody Allen, 1979, USA)
Match Point (Woody Allen, 2005, USA)
Mildred Pierce (Michael Curtiz, 1945, USA)
Mother India (Mehboob Khan, 1957, India)
The Naked Island (Kaneto Shindo, 1960, Japan)
The New World (Terrence Malick, 2005, USA)
Niagara (Henry Hathaway, 1953, USA)
Night Moves (Kelly Reichardt, 2013, USA)
Obsession (Luchino Visconti, 1943, Italy)
On Dangerous Ground (Nicholas Ray, 1951, USA)
Once Upon a Time in Anatolia (Nuri Bilge Ceylan, 2011, Turkey)
Paisan (Roberto Rossellini, 1946, Italy)
Persona (Ingmar Bergman, 1966, Sweden)
Pierrot le fou (Jean-Luc Godard, 1965, France)
Pigs and Battleships (Shohei Imamura, 1961, Japan)
Platform (Jia Zhangke, 2000, China)
Predator (John McTiernan, 1987, USA)
Profound Desires of the Gods (Shohei Imamura, 1968, Japan)
Purple Noon (René Clément, 1960, France)
Rules of the Game (Jean Renoir, 1939, France)
Saturday Night and Sunday Morning (Karel Reisz, 1960, UK)
*The Seven Samurai (*Akira Kurosawa, 1954, Japan)
Splash (Ron Howard, 1984, USA)
Spring, Summer, Fall, Winter...and Spring (Kim Ki-duk, 2003, South Korea/
    Germany)
Stagecoach (John Ford, 1939, USA)
Stalker (Andrei Tarkovsky, 1979, Soviet Union)
Still Life (Jia Zhangke, 2006, China)
Still the Water (Naomi Kawase, 2014, Japan)
Strange Days (Kathryn Bigelow, 1995, USA)
Stromboli (Roberto Rossellini, 1950, Italy)
Sunrise: A Song of Two Humans (F. W. Murnau, 1927, USA)

The Tale of Iya (Tetsuichiro Tsuta, 2013, Japan)

Terminator 2 (James Cameron, 1991, USA)

The Texas Chainsaw Massacre (Tobe Hooper, 1974, USA)

Thirty Leagues Under the Sea (John Ernest Williamson, 1914, USA)

This Happy Breed (David Lean, 1944, UK)

Through the Olive Trees (Abbas Kiarostami, 1994, Iran)

Titanic (James Cameron, 1997, USA)

Tokyo Story (Yasujiro Ozu, 1953, Japan)

The Travelling Players (Theodoros Angelopoulos, 1975, Greece)

Two-Lane Blacktop (Monte Hellman, 1971, USA)

Uncle Boonmee Who Can Recall His Past Lives (Apichatpong Weerasethakul, 2010, Thailand)

Vagabond (Agnès Varda, 1985, France)

Vertigo (Alfred Hitchcock, 1958, USA)

Weekend (Jean-Luc Godard, 1967, France)

When Clouds Clear (Danielle Bernstein and Anne Slick, 2008, USA/Ecuador)

Where Is My Friend's House? (Abbas Kiarostami, 1987, Iran)

Wild River (Elia Kazan, 1960, USA)

Wild Strawberries (Ingmar Bergman, 1957, Sweden)

The Wind (Victor Sjöström, 1928, USA)

Yellow Earth (Chen Kaige, 1984, China)

Yojimbo (Akira Kurosawa, 1961, Japan)

You Only Live Once (Fritz Lang, 1937, USA)

Young Mr. Lincoln (John Ford, 1939, USA)

Zabriskie Point (Michelangelo Antonioni, 1970, Italy)

BIBLIOGRAPHY

Adorno, Theodor (1997 [1970]) *Aesthetic Theory*, ed. Rolf Tiedemann, trans. Gretel Adorno. London and New York: Bloomsbury.

Affron, Charles and Mirella Jona Affron (1995) *Sets in Motion: Art Direction and Film Narrative*. New Brunswick, NJ: Rutgers University Press.

Andrew, Dudley (1978) *André Bazin*. Oxford: Oxford University Press.

Bawarshi, Anis (2001) 'The Ecology of Genre', in Christian R. Weisser and Sidney L. Dobrin (eds) *Ecocomposition: Theoretical and Pedagogical Approaches*. Albany, NY: State University of New York Press, 69–80.

Bazin, André (1967) *What is Cinema? Volume I*, trans. Hugh Gray. Berkeley, CA: University of California Press.

____ (1971) *What is Cinema? Volume II*, trans. Hugh Gray. Berkeley, CA: University of California Press.

Bell, Jonathan F. (2000) 'Shadows in the Hinterland: Rural Noir', in Mark Lamster (ed.) *Architecture and Film*. New York: Princeton Architectural Press, 217–230.

Berque, Augustin (1997) *Japan: Nature, Artifice and Japanese Culture*, trans. Ros Schwartz. Yelvertoft Manor: Pilkington.

Biesen, Sheri Chinen (2005) *Blackout: World War II and the Origins of Film Noir*. Baltimore, MD: Johns Hopkins University Press.

Bíró, Yvette (2008) *Turbulence and Flow in Film: The Rhythmic Design*, trans. Paul Salaman. Bloomington, IN: Indiana University Press.

Bordwell, David and Kristin Thompson (2001) *Film Art: An Introduction*, 6th edn. New York: McGraw Hill.

Bousé, Derek (2000) *Wildlife Films*. Philadelphia, PA: University of Pennsylvania Press.

Bozak, Nadia (2011) *The Cinematic Footprint: Lights, Camera, Natural Resources*. New Brunswick, NJ: Rutgers University Press.

Braudy, Leo (1998) 'The Genre of Nature', in Nick Browne (ed.) *Refiguring American Film Genres: History and Theory*. Berkeley, CA: University of California Press, 278–310.

___ (2002 [1976]) *The World in a Frame: What We See in Films*, 2nd edn. Chicago: University of Chicago Press.

Brereton, Pat (2005) *Hollywood Utopia: Ecology in Contemporary American Cinema*. Bristol: Intellect.

___ (2015) *Environmental Ethics and Film*. New York: Routledge.

Brown, William (2013) *Supercinema: Film-Philosophy for the Digital Age*. New York: Berghahn.

Buell, Lawrence (2001) *Writing for an Endangered World: Literature, Culture, and Environment in the United States and Beyond*. Harvard, MA: Harvard University Press.

Burch, Noël (1979) *To the Distant Observer: Form and Meaning in the Japanese Cinema*. Berkely, CA: University of California Press.

Cain, James M. (1934) *The Postman Always Rings Twice*. London: Orion.

Canudo, Ricciotto (1993 [1923]) 'Reflections on the Seventh Art', in Richard Abel (ed.) *French Film Theory and Criticism: A History/Anthology, 1907–1939*. Princeton, NJ: Princeton University Press, 291–303.

Carmichael, Deborah A. (2006) 'Introduction', in Deborah A. Carmichael (ed.) *The Landscape of Hollywood Westerns*. Salt Lake City, UT: University of Utah Press, 1–16.

Casetti, Francesco (2008) *Eye of the Century: Film, Experience, Modernity*, trans. Erin Larkin and Jennifer Pranolo. New York: Columbia University Press.

Casey, Edward S. (2003) 'Taking a Glance at the Environment: Preliminary Thoughts on a Promising Topic', in Charles S. Brown and Ted Toadvine (ed.) *Eco-Phenomenology: Back to the Earth Itself*. Albany, NY: State University of New York Press, 187–210.

Cavell, Stanley (2005) 'A Capra Moment', in William Rotham (ed.) *Cavell on Film*. Albany, NY: State University of New York Press, 135–44.

Clayton, Alex and Andrew Klevan (2011) 'Introduction: The Language and Style of Film Criticism', in Alex Clayton and Andrew Klevan (eds) *The

Language and Style of Film Criticism. London: Routledge.

Danto, Arthur C. (2001) *Philosophizing Art: Selected Essays*. Berkeley, CA: University of California Press.

Deleuze, Gilles (2004) *Desert Islands and Other Texts: 1953–1974*, ed. David Lapoujade, trans. Michael Taormina. Los Angeles: Semiotext(e).

____ (2005) *Cinema 2: The Time-Image*, trans. Hugh Tomlinson. London: Continuum.

Desser, David (2003) 'Global Noir: Genre Film in the Age of Transnationalism', in Barry Keith Grant (ed.) *Film Genre Reader III*. Austin, TX: University of Texas Press, 516–36.

Donaldson, Lucy Fife (2014) *Texture in Film*. Basingstoke: Palgrave Macmillan.

Drobin, Sidney I. and Sean Morey (eds) (2009) *Ecosee: Image, Rhetoric, Nature, Greening the Media*. Albany, NY: State University of New York Press.

Durgnat, Raymond (1996 [1970]) 'Paint it Black: The Family Tree of Film Noir', in Alain Silver and James Ursini (eds) *Film Noir Reader*. New York: Limelight Editions, 37–52.

Eisenstein, Sergei (1949) *Film Form: Essays in Film Theory*, trans. Jay Leyda. San Diego, CA: Harcourt.

____ (1987) *Nonindifferent Nature: Film and the Structure of Things*, trans. Herbert Marshall. Cambridge: Cambridge University Press.

Emerson, Ralph Waldo (2003) *Nature and Selected Essays*, ed. Larzer Ziff. New York: Penguin.

Epstein, Jean (1981 [1924]) 'On Certain Characteristics of Photogénie', trans. Tom Milne. *AfterImage*, 10, 20–3.

Forns-Broggi, Roberto (2013) 'Ecocinema and "Good Life" in Latin America', in Tommy Gustafsson and Pietari Kääpä (eds) *Transnational Ecocinema: Film Culture in an Era of Ecological Transformation*. Bristol: Intellect, 185–200.

Frow, John (2006) *Genre: The New Critical Idiom*. London and New York: Routledge.

Garrard, Greg (2004) *Ecocriticism*. London and New York: Routledge.

Goodman, Nelson (1978) *Ways of Worldmaking*. New York: Hackett.

Gustafsson, Henrik (2013) 'A Wet Emptiness: The Phenomenology of Film Noir', in Andrew Spicer and Helen Hanson (eds) *A Companion to Film Noir*. Bognor Regis: Wiley-Blackwell, 50–66.

Handyside, Fiona (2014) *Cinema at the Shore: The Beach in French Film*. Bern: Peter Lang.

Harding, Colin and Simon Popple (1996) *In the Kingdom of Shadows: A Companion to Early Cinema*. London: Cygnus Arts.

Harootunian, Harry D. (2000) *Overcome by Modernity: History, Culture, and Community in Interwar Japan*. Princeton, NJ: Princeton University Press.

Higson, Andrew (1984) 'Space, Place, Spectacle: Landscape and Townscape in the Kitchen Sink Film', *Screen*, 25, 4–5, 2–21.

Hoberman, J. (2004) 'Coal Miners' Slaughter', *The Village Voice*, 20 January. On-line. Available at: https://www.villagevoice.com/2004/01/20/coal-miners-slaughter/ (accessed 31 August 2017).

Ingram, David (2000) *Green Screen: Environmentalism and Hollywood Cinema*. Exeter: University of Exeter Press.

Ivakhiv, Adrian (2013) *Ecologies of the Moving Image: Cinema, Affect, Nature, Environmental Humanities*. Waterloo, ON: Wilfred Laurier University Press.

Jameson, Frederic (2016) *Raymond Chandler: The Detections of Totality*. London: Verso.

Jones, Kent (1999) *L'Argent*. London: British Film Institute.

Kaplan, E. Ann (1998) *Women in Film Noir,* 2nd edn. London: British Film Institute.

Keathley, Christian (2006) *Cinephilia and History, or, The Wind in the Trees*. Bloomington, IN: Indiana University Press.

Ko, Mika (2013) *Japanese Cinema and Otherness: Nationalism, Multiculturalism and the Problem of Japaneseness*. Abingdon: Routledge.

Koren, Leonard (2008) *Wabi-sabi for Artists, Designers, Poets & Philosophers*. Point Reyes, CA: Imperfect.

Kovacs, András Bálint (2007) *Screening Modernism: European Art Cinema, 1950–1980*. Chicago: University of Chicago Press.

Kracauer, Siegfried (1960) *Theory of Film: Redemption of Physical Reality*. Oxford: Oxford University Press.

Lee, Maggie (2014) 'Still the Water', *Variety*, 20 May. On-line. Available at: http://variety.com/2014/film/asia/cannes-film-review-still-the-water-1201186839/ (accessed 29 August 2017).

Lefebvre, Martin (2006) 'Between Setting and Landscape in the Cinema', in Martin Lefebvre (ed.) *Landscape and Cinema*. New York: Routledge, 19–60.

Leung, Helen Hok-Sze (2003) '*Yellow Earth*: Hesitant Apprenticeship and Bitter Agency', in Chris Berry (ed.) *Chinese Films in Focus*. London: British Film Institute, 191–7.

Lott, Eric (1997) 'The Whiteness of Film Noir', *American Literary History*, 9, 542–66.

Lu, Sheldon and Jiayin Mi (eds) (2009) *Chinese Ecocinema in the Age of Environmental Challenge*. Hong Kong: Hong Kong University Press.

Marshall, Tim (2015) *Prisoners of Geography: Ten Maps That Tell You Everything You Need to Know About Global Politics*. London: Elliott & Thompson.

Mayer, Sophie (2014) '"Gutta cavat lapidem": The Sonorous Politics of Lucrecia Martel's Swimming Pools', in Christopher Brown and Pam Hirsch (eds) *The Cinema of the Swimming Pool*. Bern: Peter Lang, 191–202.

McKibben, Bill (2003 [1989]) *The End of Nature: Humanity, Climate Change and the Natural World*. London: Bloomsbury.

McKim, Kristi (2013) *Cinema as Weather: Stylistic Screens and Atmospheric Change*. New York: Routledge.

Mellen, Joan (1976) *The Waves at Genji's Door: Japan Through its Cinema*. New York: Pantheon.

Minghelli, Giuliana (2008) 'Haunted Frames: History and Landscape in Luchino Visconti's *Ossessione*', *Italica*, 85, 2, 173–96.

Mitchell, W. J. T. (2002) 'Imperial Landscape', in W. J. T. Mitchell (ed.) *Power and Landscape*. Chicago: Chicago University Press, 5–34.

Monani, Salma and Matthew Beehr (2011) 'John Sayles' *Honeydripper*: African Americans and the Environment', *ISLE: Interdisciplinary Studies in Literature and Environment*, 18, 1, 5–25.

Morgan, Daniel (2013) *Late Godard and the Possibilities of Cinema*. Berkeley, CA: University of California Press.

Mules, Warwick (2014) *With Nature: Nature Philosophy as Poetics Through Schelling, Heidegger, Benjamin and Nancy*. Bristol: Intellect.

Mulvey, Laura (2006) *Death 24x a Second: Stillness and the Moving Image*. London: Reaktion.

Münsterberg, Hugo (2002 [1916]) *Hugo Münsterberg on Film: The Photoplay: A Psychological Study and Other Writings*, ed. Allan Langdale. London and New York: Routledge.

Murray, Robin L. and Joseph K. Heumann (2009) *Ecology and Popular Film*:

Cinema on the Edge. Albany, NY: State University of New York Press.

____ (2012*) Gunfight at the Eco-Corral: Western Cinema and the Environment*. Norman, OK: University of Oklahoma Press.

Nagib, Lúcia (2011) *World Cinema and the Ethics of Realism*. New York: Continuum.

Neale, Steve (2003) *Genre and Hollywood*. London and New York: Routledge.

Orr, John (1998) *Contemporary Cinema*. Edinburgh: Edinburgh University Press.

Palmer, Tim (2010) 'The Rules of the World: Japanese Ecocinema and Kiyoshi Kurosawa', in Paula Willoquet-Maricondi (ed.) *Framing the World: Explorations in Ecocriticism and Film*. Charlottesville, VA: University of Virginia Press, 209–24.

Perkins, V. F. (1972*) Film as Film: Understanding and Judging Movies*. Harmondsworth: Penguin.

Pick, Anat and Guinevere Narraway (eds) (2013) *Screening Nature: Cinema Beyond the Human*. New York: Berghahn.

Pomerance, Murray (2008) *The Horse Who Drank the Sky: Film Experience Beyond Narrative and Theory*. New Brunswick, NJ: Rutgers University Press.

Purse, Lisa (2013) *Digital Imaging in Popular Cinema*. Edinburgh: Edinburgh University Press.

Richardson, Carl (1992) *Autopsy: An Element of Realism in Film Noir*. Metuchen, NJ: Scarecrow Press.

Richie, Donald (1997) 'Notes for a Study on Shohei Imamura', in James Quandt (ed.) *Shohei Imamura*. Toronto, ON: Toronto International Film Festival Group, 7–43.

Rust, Stephen, Salma Monani and Sean Cubitt (eds) (2016) *Ecomedia: Key Issues*. New York: Routledge.

Schama, Simon (2004) *Landscape and Memory*. London: HarperCollins.

Schrader, Paul (1972) 'Notes on Film Noir', *Film Comment*, 8, 1, 8–13.

Shakespeare, William (1991) *King Lear*. John F. Andrews (ed.). London: Everyman.

Shiel, Mark (2012) *Hollywood Cinema and the Real Los Angeles*. London: Reaktion.

Shigehiko, Hasumi (1997) 'Sunny Skies', in David Desser (ed.) *Tokyo Story*, trans. Kathy Shigeta. Cambridge: Cambridge University Press, 118–30.

Shirane, Haruo (2012) *Japan and the Culture of the Four Seasons: Nature, Literature, and the Arts*. New York: Columbia University Press.

Sitney, P. Adams (1993) 'Landscape in the Cinema: The Rhythms of the World and the Camera', in Salim Kemal and Ivan Gaskell (eds) *Landscape, Natural Beauty and the Arts*. Cambridge, MA: Cambridge University Press, 103–26.

Sobchack, Vivian (1998) '"Lounge Time": Post-War Crises and the Chronotope of Film Noir', in Nick Browne (ed.) *Refiguring American Film Genres: History and Theory*. Berkeley, CA: University of California Press, 129–70.

Soper, Kate (1995) *What is Nature?: Culture, Politics and the Non-Human*. London: Wiley-Blackwell.

Spicer, Andrew (2007) 'Introduction', in Andrew Spicer (ed.) *European Film Noir*. Manchester: Manchester University Press, 1–22.

Spirn, Anne Whiston (1998) *The Language of Landscape*. New Haven, CT: Yale University Press.

Stam, Robert (2000) *Film Theory: An Introduction*. Oxford: Blackwell.

Starosielski, Nicole (2013) 'Beyond Fluidity: A Cultural History of Cinema Under Water', in Stephen Rust, Salma Monani and Sean Cubitt (eds) *Ecocinema Theory and Practice*. New York: Routledge, 149–68.

Thomas, Deborah (1992) 'Psychoanalysis and Film Noir', in Ian Cameron (ed.) *The Movie Book of Film Noir*. London: Studio Vista, 71–87.

Toles, George (2012) '"Cocoon of Fire": Awakening to Love in Murnau's *Sunrise*', *Film International*, 9, 6, 8–29.

Whissel, Kristen (2014) *Spectacular Digital Effects: CGI and Contemporary Cinema*. Durham, NC: Duke University Press.

Williams, Raymond (2014 [1976]) *Keywords: A Vocabulary of Culture and Society*. London: Fourth Estate.

Wilson, George (1986) *Narration in Light: Studies in Cinematic Point of View*. Baltimore, MD: Johns Hopkins University Press.

Wood, Michael (2012a) 'At the Movies', *London Review of Books*, 34, 9, 10 May, 18.

_____ (2012b) *Film: A Very Short Introduction*. Oxford: Oxford University Press.

Yacavone, Daniel (2014) *Film Worlds: A Philosophical Aesthetics of Cinema*. New York: Columbia University Press.

Young, Vernon (1963) 'Films to Confirm the Poets', *The Hudson Review*, 16, 2, 255–64.

Žižek, Slavoj (1990) 'The Thing from Inner Space: On Tarkovsky', *Angelaki*, 4, 3, 221–31.

INDEX